Fau : Portrait of an Ethiopian Famine

For my father
who taught me honesty, patience, and kindness
and for my mother
who taught me compassion

F A U

Portrait of an Ethiopian Famine

by
James Waller

McFarland & Company, Inc., Publishers
Jefferson, North Carolina, and London

British Library Cataloguing-in-Publication data are available

Library of Congress Cataloguing-in-Publication Data

Waller, James, 1955–
    Fau : portrait of an Ethiopian famine / James Waller.
      p. cm.
    [Includes index.]
    Includes bibliographical references.
    ISBN 0-89950-515-5 (sewn softcover : 55# alk. paper) ∞
    1. Refugees—Sudan. 2. Refugees—Ethiopia. 3. Famines—Ethiopia.
  I. Title.
  HV640.4.S73W35   1990
  362.8'0963—dc20   89-43636
                                                   CIP

Manufactured in the United States of America

McFarland & Company, Inc., Publishers
  Box 611, Jefferson, North Carolina 28640

Acknowledgments

I am in debt to a great many people for their support and assistance in the preparation of this book. I am especially grateful to Ian Timm, who permitted me access to IRC files, and to Barbara Smith, Dr. Carol Beechy, Ben Curran, Karl and Sue Schlotterbeck, Dr. Peter Krewet, Richard Swenson, and Mike McCracken for their contributions, suggestions, and encouragement. I am also indebted to Tadella Aberaha of REST and to Yohannes Hiwot, Haile Micael, and Abie Girma — good friends who aided me both personally and professionally during my 18 months in the Sudan.

Contents

I. Goay Gabrehewit   1

Short biography of Goay Gabrehewit, one of the Fau refugees, ending as she prepares to leave Ethiopia for the Sudan in search of food.

II. Kasai Maskal   9

How Kasai Maskal abandoned his study of the priesthood at the holy city of Axum to help lead his people out of Ethiopia to the Sudan.
The ancient religious history of Ethiopia.

III. Ngistie Abraha   15

Ngistie Abraha's flight to the Sudan and her first two months at the Sudanese famine relief camp at Tuklebab.

IV. Background   21

Ethiopia's internal politics and the international response since the cycle of drought began in the early 1970s.
The migration of famine victims to the Sudan beginning in October 1984.

V. Tuklebab   37

The disaster that occurred at Tuklebab reception center because of a lack of water, food, and medicine (October–December 1984).

Introduction

Three successive years of crop failures led to the great Ethiopian famine of 1984–85. In October 1984, the first groups of what eventually grew to be 300,000 Ethiopians migrated into the deserts of neighboring Sudan in search of food. The first 40,000 of these refugees found themselves in a dusty relief camp near the Sudanese town of El Fau. At Fau, they suffered loss, death, and misery, but with the aid of international relief efforts, a process of healing was begun. On February 25, 1986, after a 16-month odyssey, the survivors recrossed the desert to their homes with health restored and hope renewed.

This book deals with the Ethiopian famine in a broad, historical sense, but focuses its attentions primarily on the 40,000 refugees at Fau as a microcosm — a portrait of the famine.

The International Rescue Committee (IRC), a New York–based voluntary agency, ran the largest relief operations in the Sudan for Ethiopian refugees; included in its responsibilities were the medical and public health programs at Fau. I arrived at Fau in the employ of IRC in January 1985 — early enough to witness the arrivals of the last groups of incoming refugees. I set up field laboratories for the diagnosis of malaria, tuberculosis, and other infectious diseases; later, I was put in charge of IRC's public health programs at Fau.

While most of the other relief workers stayed at the camp from three to six months, I lived and worked at Fau for 1½ years. This extended stay meant that I was the only field worker to be present at the Fau refugee camp from the beginning to the end; to see the arrival of the refugees at Fau, the death and desolation of the early months, the establishment of medical and feeding programs, the refugees' gradual return to health, and finally the dismantling of the camp and the refugees' departure back to Ethiopia.

It may be asked whether the international relief efforts directed towards starving Ethiopians in 1984 and 1985 could have been more timely to prevent the tragedy of mass starvation. But such efforts require the support of key individuals, governments, and world public opinion. Perhaps the greater tragedy is that it took the spectacle of mass starvation to motivate the public sympathy which could have prevented the disaster in the first place.

Recrimination should not, however, cast any shadow over the successful, heroic efforts that transformed death and despair in the camps into life and hope. The purpose of *Fau* is to show that, despite the myriad difficulties in implementing relief operations under such circumstances as existed, people of good intentions can prevail to succeed, and that grief, and even death, can be overcome by the strength of people helping each other.

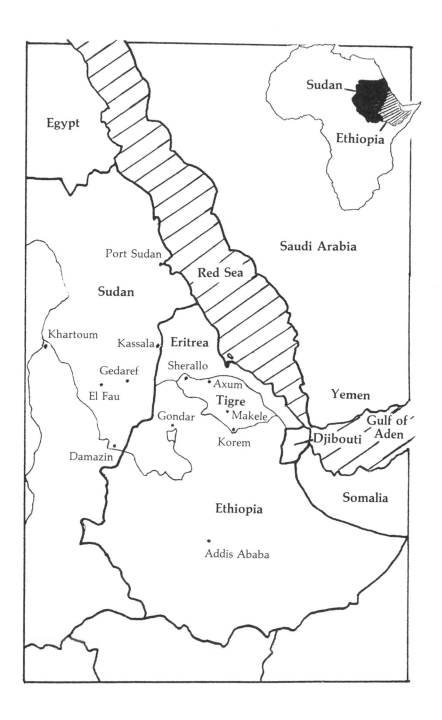

Northeast Africa

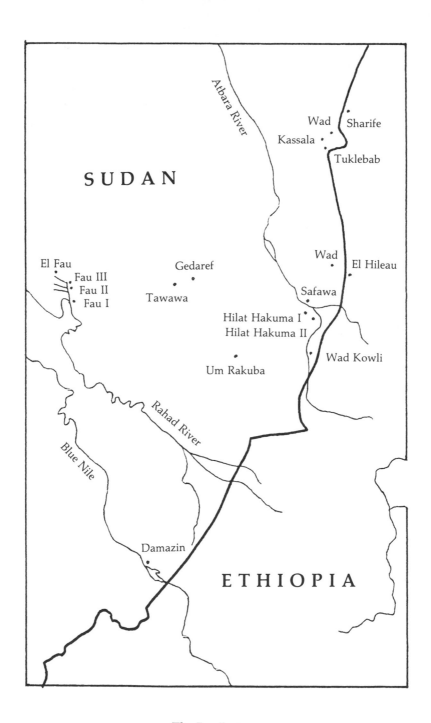

The Fau Region

I. Goay Gabrehewit

Tigre Province, Ethiopia, October 1984: Goay Gabrehewit sat on the rocky soil on the outskirts of the village of Sherallo. She pulled her knees up to her chin and shook her body in an effort to stop the continuous sobs of the past two days. The morning was cold and she drew her *gabi,* or long shawl, a little closer over her shoulders. The grey streaks of dawn lightened the skies above the hilltops as she pulled herself to her feet. Today she would make the final preparations for her journey to the Sudan. The normal grieving rituals that accompany the death of a child would have to be curtailed.

As she wrapped her bundles in coarse, white cotton cloth, her remaining four children began to stir. She glanced at them huddled together under a blanket on the cold ground. Then she thought of the three-year-old whom she had laid in the ground two days earlier. She had also been wrapped in coarse, white cotton cloth. Goay dropped her work and covered her mouth with her hand. What had happened to her life — a life that until five years ago had been so content? Since then it seemed that one calamity had followed on another. What had happened?

Goay grew up in a small village called Nadir in central Tigre Province. Like nearly all the families in Nadir, hers lived off the land as farmers. For most of her childhood she lived with her mother and father, a widowed grandmother, two aunts who had never married, four brothers and two sisters. The farm was medium-sized and the family was comfortable economically in that there was always an excess of "dagusa" and "teff" (two sorghum-like crops) and wheat to sell to the market in nearby Shillaro town.

1

When Goay was 15, her father died. A year and a half later, Goay married Haile Mariam, a man with whom she had been acquainted for several years. Most marriages in Tigre are between people of the same village, and with Nadir being so small, approximately 1,000 inhabitants, nearly everyone knew everybody else.

Arrangements for the marriage had been delicate, complicated by the death of Goay's father and by the fact that Haile's family held far less land than Goay's. Haile's parents spent several sessions with Nadir's nine *shimagali,* or village elders. The elders, in turn, spent many long hours with Goay's mother and four elder brothers.

In Tigre, the families of the bride and groom never negotiate directly, but accomplish the marriage arrangements through the village elders. The village elders act as arbiters in any dispute and are involved in all community activities. Decisions are reached by consensus of all the parties involved, and that is why the decision-making process often seems interminable. One of the village elders, though he holds no special title, holds more authority than the others, and his judgment almost always is the determining influence in case of a deadlock.

Shortly after their marriage, Haile convinced Goay to come with him to Addis Ababa, Ethiopia's capital city. Once in Addis, he found work as an apprentice to an electrician. He learned the skill quickly and soon was making an extraordinary income. Within a year of their marriage, Goay bore their first child.

Over the next several years, Goay and Haile had three more children and accumulated five homes in Addis Ababa, a small farm outside of town, and a little shop that was managed by Goay. The homes they owned were modest, including the one in which they resided. It comprised three rooms and was made of brick. It had electricity and running water, but lacked the luxuries of a refrigerator or television. Such appliances were not really viewed as necessities by Goay; fresh meats and vegetables were sold in the nearby open markets, and entertainment for her was best accomplished by gathering with family and friends.

Goay worked in her shop from early in the morning until about seven o'clock at night — not of necessity, but for the satisfaction of performing a good day's work. The main items for sale in the shop were beans, sugar, onions, tea, and coffee. The growing and brewing of coffee first originated in Ethiopia in the vicinity of Kaffa, the town for which the drink is named. Coffee has been the country's leading trade and export commodity for ages. Goay sold the beans fresh; her customers would grind and roast the beans in their homes in the centuries-old coffee ceremony. When Goay returned home from the shop in the evening, there was a servant girl on hand to prepare the evening meal and to clean the utensils.

Goay had indeed been content with her life during her eight years in Addis Ababa. The revolutionary government, or Dergue, which had come to power through the deposition of Haile Selassie in 1974, had seized some of their properties in early 1979, but their losses were less than those of some of their friends. The government's communistic policies were a nuisance, but only a minor intrusion into their lives.

Late in 1979, the family boarded a bus to Tigre Province to visit parents and relatives. It was their first trip home since moving to Addis Ababa eight years earlier. The visit was intended to last six or eight weeks. They did not know they would never return to Addis.

Fighting had intensified between the Tigrean People's Liberation Front (TPLF) and the government forces in eastern Tigre. The TPLF controlled the roads within Tigre, but in effect the roads that connected Tigre to the rest of Ethiopia were closed — passenger buses no longer serviced the route and private cars were practically nonexistent. They could have taken the chance of returning to Addis on foot, but such a journey would take at least two weeks, and with four small children in the company, this was an unlikely prospect. Besides, as Tigreans, they might be harassed by any government troops they happened across, and as Tigreans traveling to Addis, they might be mistreated by any TPLF fighters they encountered. Better to wait until the situation improved.

The months wore on, but the prospect of returning to Addis grew dimmer and dimmer. Haile acquired a small parcel of land from his father, and the two of them worked to raise dhura, white teff, and beans. The whole family lived in one room under a roof of straw in a house made of stone. To Goay, the little village of Nadir seemed even smaller than when she was a girl, and the change in the family's fortunes put a tremendous strain on her marriage.

A year after their arrival in Nadir, Goay's mother died, not quite 50 years old, exhausted by hard work and a hard life.

Following the death of her mother, Goay's marriage with Haile

grew further strained. Nevertheless, a fifth child was born in early
1981. Six months later came separation and divorce. The Nadir
shimagali settled the divorce — the same men who had arranged the
marriage 10 years earlier.

After her divorce, Goay and the five children moved into her
eldest brother's home. He gave her some land, which she in turn
rented to a tenant farmer for half of the harvested crop, a common
tenant arrangement in Tigre.

In 1982, the crops in the area failed because of drought. The
grain Goay collected from her tenant farmer was a pitiful amount.
Not wanting to be a burden to her brothers, Goay took her three
youngest children and walked three days to Shillaro town to find
work.

Shillaro was bigger than Nadir, having about 3,000 people, and
the houses were less scattered than at Nadir. Goay moved in with a
distant cousin and began to earn a living preparing local beer and
whiskey. The work demanded long hours, and the customers were
sometimes rude and belligerent, but at least there was plenty to eat
in Shillaro, and Goay was able to send packages of foodstuffs to
her older children and her brother's family with travelers passing
through to Nadir.

Goay stayed in Shillaro nearly two years, walking back to visit
her older children every two or three months. The rains failed again
in 1983. The food shortages of the year before were nothing compared to those of 1983. By May, fruits and vegetables were scarce
even in Shillaro market; shortages of onions, beans, and grain were
acute. By September, prices were so high that to purchase only two
pounds of tomatoes cost nearly a week's earnings.

Goay and her children ate a flat, unleavened, fermented bread
made from teff or sorghum called *enjura.* In the mornings, they ate
the enjura by itself or with hot peppers or onions; in the evenings,
they ate it with potatoes, beans, or lentils. Meat was a great luxury,
served only on holidays in small amounts; even then Goay ate none
for herself, but gave it to her children. It was small consolation that
everyone else in Shillaro was foraging for food as well.

In the winter of 1983, Goay returned to Shillaro from a visit to
her brother's home in Nadir to find that government planes had
bombed the town, and the ensuing fires had burned down her shop
and home. Perhaps because of her years in Addis Ababa, Goay had

always been neutral politically; she had never gotten involved in the Tigrean People's Liberation Movement which was central to the lives of so many of her neighbors. But now she hated the Dergue for what it had done. Life had already become so difficult; what was the point of this?

Now Goay left all five of her children at her brother's home in Nadir. She found work in a village called Aterga, a two days' walk. The village contained only about 1,000 people, and Goay found work on a farm separating chaff from grain. As payment, she was allowed to keep one-fifth of the grain.

Hard, hard times. Food became scarcer than ever before. It got so that Goay often skipped her morning meal; in the evenings, she ate her enjura with lentils. Once in a while she ate red or white beans. Onions, potatoes, and spices were no longer affordable. Tomatoes and other vegetables were no longer available at any price.

The people of the village talked incessantly about government warplanes bombing nearby villages. The most widespread rumor was of a church being shelled on a Sunday and the entire congregation being killed. Goay knew how such stories were greatly exaggerated by her countrymen, but she was afraid nonetheless. She had seen one plane fly directly over Aterga. It had circled and disappeared without doing any harm, but she was all the more afraid for having seen it. What if the planes should come to Nadir? How could she protect her children?

By June and July of 1984, it was apparent that the devastating drought was continuing into its third year. In a normal year in Ethiopia, light rains begin in early June and become heavy and frequent in July, continuing through August and on into September. It had sprinkled a few times in 1982 and 1983, enough to produce partial harvests in some areas. It sprinkled a few times in July 1984 as well, but any crops that did grow were decimated by a triple infestation of grasshoppers, weevils, and black caterpillar-like worms.

By September and October, the drought and insect plague had done their terrible work. Where food was available, prices soared. For a time, the price of meat actually fell as farmers slaughtered their livestock rather than feed them precious grain. Those farmers who had stores of grain were unwilling to sell. Low quality bread infested with weevils was the usual fare, and for the poorer of the villages, even these meager rations were hard to come by. Panic in the villages spread as rapidly as hunger.

The rumors of bombings in nearby villages persisted, and Goay was frightened for her children in Nadir. The people of Aterga began talking about leaving the village and traveling west to the Sudan to find food. There was no point in traveling east or south to government-controlled areas, or to the north to Eritrea where there was no more food than in Tigre.

In September, two representatives from the Relief Society of Tigre (REST) came to visit Aterga. The group REST is a humanitarian organization internal to Tigre Province under the umbrella of the Tigrean People's Liberation Front (TPLF), the secessionist military movement. The two men from REST, who appeared to be in their early 20s, told the villagers of Aterga that there would be an evacuation of people from Sherallo, a larger town, only a few hours' walk from Aterga. Members of REST would organize the evacuation and would take anyone who wanted to leave into the Sudan. They would travel northwest by foot and by truck to the Sudanese town of Kassala where, the men promised, international aid agencies would give food and assistance to the people. In the meantime, REST was working to ensure that food would be brought directly into Tigre from the international agencies. The journey to the Sudan would be difficult and would take two to three weeks for those who walked. There were sufficient dirt roads for most of the journey, and food would be provided at rest stops along the way. The evacuation would begin in two weeks.

The village buzzed after the visit from REST. It took Goay only a day to make up her mind. She would go to the Sudan, away from the famine and the warplanes. One of her sisters had moved to the Sudan seven years ago, and her infrequent letters suggested a good life there. Goay would go to find her; she planned never to return to Tigre.

She walked to Nadir and talked the situation over with her brother and other relatives. She left Nadir with her five children, her brother and his wife, and the four youngest of their eight children. Her brother planned to return immediately to Tigre to take care of the farm while the others were away. They walked to Sherallo through the cool, high hills, through papaya and tangerine groves whose trees no longer bore leaves. It seemed that all the vegetation was dead or dying—and this the time of year when everything should be green!

Eventually the entire population of Nadir deserted the village; Goay was among the first to leave.

About 400 people gathered in Sherallo, sleeping outside, awaiting the day of departure to the Sudan. Some put up makeshift grass shelters; most, like Goay, slept under starry African skies with only a blanket for warmth.

Several members of REST were present in Sherallo. They talked to the people in groups of 50 to 100, explaining to them about the journey they were about to undertake. About 3,000 people were already en route; this group was not the first. Only one lorry truck was available for the group, and it could carry only 40 people on its open bed. REST would decide who was eligible to ride on the back of the lorry: pregnant women, the very old, and children too small to walk. All the others must walk. Among the walkers, the strong were expected to carry those who fell ill en route. The only food available along the way at this time was enjura and lentils.

The day after they arrived in Sherallo, Goay's youngest daughter became ill with severe diarrhea and a fever. Because of a prolonged daily diet of only a few mouthfuls of enjura, the child had grown weaker and weaker over the past few weeks. The promise of more food had led Goay to leave Tigre, but now, before the journey had even begun, her youngest had fallen sick as a result of her malnourished condition.

Three days passed, and more people joined the group from neighboring villages. In the meantime, Goay's three-year-old showed no sign of improvement. She wouldn't eat and lately refused to take even water. When she did drink water, she vomited almost immediately. Because of her fever, Goay kept her wrapped up closely in a small blanket, the customary treatment for fever among Tigrean villagers.

That night, as the wind brushed her face like the passing of an angel, Goay awoke with a chill. The child that she held to her breast had stopped breathing. A long, loud, terrible wail welled up inside her and erupted from her lips. The last thing she remembers of that night was the haunting, rhythmic wailing cries of the other women in the group echoing her own in the traditional expression of shared grief.

II. Kasai Maskal

Kasai Maskal stopped for a moment to wipe the sweat from his brow. The ground was hard and rocky. The grave he was digging would have to be shallower than he had hoped. A young woman had died last night. The sun was just up now and soon the men would bear the body to the gravesite. The death had caused a stir among the people: Other than some weakness, she had not seemed ill during the walk yesterday. Kasai knew the woman's husband, and he shared in his friend's sorrow.

Only about 100 people had left Sherallo yesterday. They formed a fairly small group, but they expected to pick up many more along the way. Later in the evening they had been joined by a Bedford lorry carrying about 50 others.

The burial ceremony was kept short. Kasai whispered the words along with the priest as he assisted in performing the rituals. The words were of the ancient language Ge'ez, a language derived from ancient Sabaen and Aramaic, enriched by Greek, and containing many Syriac and Hebrew words. The language is obsolete now, its words spoken only by priests during liturgical services. Having studied for the priesthood for two years, Kasai knew the words, and he knew how to perform ablutions for the dead.

Tigreans follow the Ethiopian Orthodox Christian faith. Christianity made its appearance in Ethiopia between the years 341 and 346. Two young Christians of Syrian origin, Frumentias and Adesius, who had reached the country as the result of a shipwreck, founded a Greco-Syrian Christian community there and brought about the conversion of the emperor, Ezana. Though the rites and rituals exhibit a distinct Ethiopian flavor, Christian beliefs in Ethiopia

9

parallel those of the Egyptian Coptic, Greek Orthodox and Roman Catholic churches.

Ethiopians are unique among Africans in their Judeo-Christian heritage. Their history and legends are steeped in Biblical tradition dating all the way back to the tenth century B.C. The ancient city of Axum, still in existence in Tigre Province, is believed to be the place where the Ark of the Covenant was spirited away and hidden. In northern Tigre and parts of adjoining Eritrea Province still are found communities of Jewish Ethiopians, or *Falashas* as they are called — a lost tribe of Israel, until recently all but forgotten.

According to the *Kebra-Nagast*, or "Glory of Kings," Tamrin, a merchant from Ethiopia, supplied ebony wood, red gold, and sapphires to King Solomon for the construction of the great temple at Jerusalem. At that time, Makeda, the Biblical Queen of Sheba, ruled over the Sabaen city-state of Yeha near Axum. Intrigued by the marvelous reports of Tamrin, she, with a caravan of 797 camels, mules, and asses laden with innumerable gifts, set forth to witness for herself the splendor of Solomon's kingdom.

After six months in Jerusalem,

> the queen departed to Ethiopia and she bore a son, and she called his name Menelik. And when he had come [of age], he wished to go to his father. [And the queen] sent him forth under the charge of Tamrin the merchant....
>
> And so King Solomon anointed Menelik with the holy oil of kingship.... And Menelik ... begged of Solomon a piece of the fringe of the Ark of the Covenant.... And Solomon promised to grant his desire. And Solomon summoned his counsellors and officers and said to them, "I am sending my first born son to rule in Ethiopia. Do ye also send your first born sons to be his counsellors and officers." And they obeyed the king's command.
>
> And Azariah, son of Zadok the high priest ... went to a carpenter and said to him, "Build me a raft; for we are to journey across the sea, and if the ship sink, so shall I be saved." And he gave to the carpenter the measurements of the Ark of the Covenant. And the night before they were to depart, he ... went to the temple and entered the sanctuary ... and took the Ark and put in its place the raft and covered it with the three coverings of the Ark so that none could see the change.
>
> And the next day Solomon bade Zadok take the outer covering of the Ark and bring it to him. And Solomon gave it to Menelik .... And Menelik and the first born sons of the nobles of Israel set

forth in a great train of wagons.... And when they came to the
land of Egypt, the sons of the nobles revealed to Menelik how they
had brought the Ark with them, and Menelik was filled with joy
and skipped like a young ram before the Ark. And they went on
their journey and came to Ethiopia. And Menelik ruled in Ethiopia
and his sons after him and the sons of the nobles of Israel and their
sons after them were the counsellors and officers of the kingdom.

[And Solomon, discovering the loss, despaired of pursuit
and] charged all his counsellors and officers to keep secret the loss
of the Ark of the Covenant, and so the children of Israel knew not
that it had departed. [Arnold Hugh Martin Jones and Elizabeth
Monroe, *A History of Ethiopia* (Oxford: Oxford University Press,
1968).]

Legend tells of Menelik's return to Ethiopia and his establishment of a great kingdom at Axum. History tells of settlers crossing
the Red Sea from Saba, a kingdom of the south Arabian peninsula,
and establishing villages in Ethiopia between the tenth and fifth centuries B.C.

The Sabaen settlers intermarried with the indigenous inhabitants and from this blending of cultures there gradually emerged
the historical Kingdom of Axum. By the time of Christ, Axum had
become a wealthy commercial cosmopolis and a powerful military
state controlling Red Sea trade and major caravan routes. The
kingdom reached its apogee under King Ezana during the fourth century A.D. For more than 200 years, the Axumites maintained close
communication with the churches of Constantinople and Rome. A
theological dispute at the Council of Chalcedon, an unsuccessful
military expedition against Persia, and the spread of Islam through
the Middle East and northern Africa gradually but completely cut off
Axum's contacts with the Mediterranean countries. Shut out from
the coastal areas by the Moslems, the Axumites turned inward.
Tribes further south were assimilated, the language underwent further changes, and the capital was eventually moved south to Gondar
and later, finally, to Addis Ababa.

Throughout the centuries, the Ethiopians continued to build
churches, to propagate the faith, and to follow the traditional Christian ways. The churches of the Ethiopian highlands are famous,
especially those constructed during the thirteenth century near
Lalibela. These monolithic structures were carved out of solid rock
mountains and are of such beauty that throughout the ages pilgrims

from near and far have come there to worship. The cathedral at Axsum remains the holiest shrine in Ethiopia and

> Outside the cathedral, away to the left, is the separate chapel sacred to the Tablet of Moses said to have been brought by Menelik and his companions from Jerusalem. . . . When the door is unlocked . . . a narrow vestibule is revealed, the entire wall space being covered with paintings of sacred scenes in minute detail, with figures of angels and archangels, the central figures being a representation of the Trinity. What lies behind, in the holy of holies, nobody knows. [Jean Doresse, *Ethiopia: Ancient Cities and Temples* (New York: Elek/Putnam, 1959).]

In 1982, when he was 18 years old, Kasai Maskal had left his native village of Enticho in eastern Tigre to go to Axum to study the language of the priesthood. He experienced the drought in Axum and watched the condition of his people worsen through three successive crop failures. The drought had been especially severe in 1984, the rains having failed completely. Outside of the city, for the peasants of the countryside, the situation was even worse. Kasai listened as many people, on the point of desperation, talked of leaving their homes to travel west. There simply was not enough food here and there was no other place to turn. Government feeding centers to the southeast around the town of Makele were rumored to be overcrowded, short of food, and rampant with ill-treatment of the people by government soldiers.

When Kasai first learned of expeditions to the west and the Sudan under the organization of REST, he considered joining one of the groups. He struggled with his decision. If he left Axum he might never again be able to resume his studies. But there was a great need now for able-bodied men to accompany the sick and hungry on their journey to the west. Should he give up forever his lifelong vocation of becoming a servant of God? According to Kasai, the archangel Gabriel spoke to him in a dream and directed him to relinquish the priesthood to become a servant of the people.

It had been nine days from Axum to Sherallo. This was the fourth grave that Kasai had helped dig. Every day now, there seemed a greater urgency to get on with the journey. Every night, Kasai prayed for the safe passage of his people — passage to a place where food might be plentiful as manna on their journey through the wilderness, passage to a place where he could watch his people grow and gain health and strength.

Throughout the day, Kasai sat with the husband of the young woman who had died. He hoped his words were of some comfort. He had convinced the husband to continue on with the journey in order to help support those who would grow weak as the walk progressed. There would be no time for prolonged grieving; the journey would resume as soon as dusk fell.

At about five o'clock in the afternoon, the lorry carrying children, the elderly, and those too weak to walk set out. Driving would be hazardous this evening as it was a moonless night.

About an hour after the lorry left, before the sun had even set, Kasai heard the bombs. The sound was muffled by distance, but it was distinct nonetheless. The people continued to prepare to resume their journey, but there was a perceptible uneasiness among them. Shortly after dusk the news came and the word spread rapidly — the lorry had been hit by government planes. Thirty-two people died in the bombing, eleven of them children.

Kasai ran along with several others up to the site of the bombing. His own journey would be delayed several days to dig more graves. Though he would see great suffering in the coming months, the sight before him now would remain the most horrible to his memory. As he dug the rocky soil, he recited to himself in Ge'ez the ancient prayers he had learned at Axum — prayers for the dead.

III. Ngistie Abraha

Ngistie Abraha was a 20-year-old girl with a 15-month-old daughter. She lived in a small one-room straw house with mud floors in a tiny village called Gwaro in western Tigre Province. Her husband, Zorai, worked as a farmer, but after three years of drought there was little food for the young family despite help from their parents.

In June of 1984 Ngistie gave birth to another daughter. The little baby was sick from birth and Ngistie blamed the sickness on her own bad breast milk, bad because she was not eating enough good food to produce good milk. Three weeks after her birth, the youngest daughter died never really having a chance to live.

By November 1984, famine had come to Gwaro. Many of the 200 villagers had already abandoned their homes to join the REST expeditions to the Sudan. Ngistie's parents and her husband's parents refused to leave, afraid that in leaving they would lose their property forever. They begged the young couple to remain in Gwaro. Ngistie and Zorai pleaded just as earnestly for their parents to come with them to the Sudan where there would be enough food for everyone. In the end, Ngistie and her husband took their first child and left Gwaro and their parents behind.

They expected the journey to be relatively easy. The Sudanese town of Kassala was only six or seven days away walking. They considered making the journey on their own, but with a one-and-a-half-year-old baby along, they decided to travel with a group. A big group of about 600 people and REST were camped near the village on their way to the Sudan. Ngistie and Zorai presented themselves to the REST guides and were accepted into the expedition.

Ngistie Abraha

The journey was difficult: up and down rocky hills, over stony trails, through dry forests whose thirsty trees bore few leaves, and along muddy stream beds trickling brackish, foul-smelling water. Travel was at night with only moonlight to guide the way. In the daytime they rested under the shade of thorny trees or in rocky ravines. They gathered wood with the group to build cooking fires for bread.

On the second day, early in the morning, two government planes circled in the distance. Ngistie had to shade her eyes from the rising sun in order to see them. The people scattered in panic, but the planes soon disappeared from sight, their droning engines fading in the distance.

Ngistie and Zorai remained in hiding the rest of the day as did their 600 companions. No cooking fires were allowed that day for fear that the smoke would draw attention to themselves. A few mouthfuls of leftover bread from the day before were all that sustained them till the next morning.

The morning before they were to arrive in Kassala, Zorai awoke with chills and a fever. Although mosquitoes are few, malaria is a common disease of western Tigre. Zorai had contracted a severe case. For nine days he drifted in and out of delirium. His lips split open from the parching fever while at the same time his body shivered through two heavy blankets from the chills. When he was coherent enough to talk, he cried that his head felt as if it were about to explode.

Two men from REST helped Ngistie and Zorai. They put them in a shelter made from empty wheat flour bags stitched together and tied to wooden poles. They gave Ngistie water, wheat flour, and lentils for daily meals. They explained that even though Kassala was only a day away, chloroquine antimalarial drugs were impossible to procure. They did have ORS (Oral Rehydration Solution) which they administered to Zorai to prevent further dehydration from the fever.

On the tenth day, Zorai's headache subsided, the fever and chills diminished, and his glassy eyes began to focus again. Ngistie prayed joyfully at her husband's recovery.

On the twelfth day, early in the morning, a Bedford lorry pulled into the camp with 45 people crammed onto the back. The REST member in charge of this leg of the journey, only a teenager himself, instructed Ngistie and Zorai to take their child and ride in this vehicle when it resumed its journey in the evening. He judged Zorai to be too weak to walk the 12 more hours that lay between here and Kassala. Going by lorry, they would arrive before daybreak.

Under a tree nearby were three barrels of fuel. Once evening fell, the driver emptied nearly half a barrel into his vehicle with a hand-pump. Ngistie wrapped the baby underneath her shawl and helped Zorai climb up into the back of the lorry.

The trip was terribly unpleasant — nearly 50 people, weak and ill, crammed on top of each other, stumbling, whimpering, some vomiting. The truck lurched over hills and lunged down steep inclines. It moved slowly without headlights and when its wheels ran over big rocks the slowness only intensified the bone-crushing jolts in the back.

After a while, the lorry drove on level ground for a long time. Then, with the moon still high in the sky in the dead of the night, the truck rolled to a stop. More than a year later Ngistie would remember how silent the world seemed when that noisy engine was finally shut off. One by one, the people climbed down from the back of the truck speaking not a word, as if afraid to break the silence. Tired, exhausted, each one found a spot on the cold, dusty ground and fell asleep.

In the morning, Ngistie, Zorai, and the baby were rounded up along with the others who had arrived during the night. They gave their names to some REST officials who wrote in hardbound notebooks. They were told where they could find their food rations and were given a small container for water.

Several days passed before Ngistie and Zorai could really believe that they were indeed in the Sudan, that they had reached the end of their journey. The place where they found themselves was a desolate spot about 13 miles away from the Sudanese town of Kassala and 20 miles from the Ethiopian border, barren, dusty, windy, hot in the daytime, and cold during the night.

The name of the place where Ngistie and Zorai found themselves was Tuklebab Mesa. The name in the local Sudanese dialect meant "Gate of Refuge," but there was no shelter here for any of the 20,000 Tigreans whose journey had ended here, not even canvas tents — these would appear in other refugee camps at a later date. The people sought shelter under rocks and leafless thornbushes. Many tied shirts and blankets to the branches of the few acacia trees for shade.

Telling was the lack of organizaton by or for the refugees. Control by REST was no longer as apparent as it had been during the journey; Sudanese authorities did not make their presence felt. According to Ngistie, the food distribution system was irregular at best. Disorder and confusion ruled when the drinking water supply trucks rolled in. Health workers spent most of their time burying the dead. The faces of those who had lived in this place for several weeks already were grim, hopeless, and despairing. Those hundreds who continued to arrive every night awoke to disbelief that the end of their long suffering and travels lay at this barren, dusty netherworld.

Ngistie and Zorai would spend more than two months at Tuklebab Mesa. They would remember those weeks as time spent in hell. Water was so scarce that no one washed; their clothes quickly turned to rags. Sometimes they waited days for any food at all. Some days the water trucks failed to show up. Those were the worst days: many people simply died of thirst and dehydration.

The camp's population had grown to approximately 40,000 people by Christmas. According to Ngistie, between 50 and 100 people died each day. Her own baby died three days after Christmas. Ngistie and Zorai had been unable to find a single scrap of food at all for five days—the camp had simply run out. Ngistie says her baby wasn't sick with any kind of illness; she died from hunger.

After the death of her baby, Ngistie desperately wanted to return to Tigre as so many of the other refugees were already doing. Zorai had finally agreed, but then Ngistie's sister turned up in camp and counseled against returning. There was no food left at home either, she said. Besides, she continued, REST had promised to bring in the Red Cross and other foreigners to take care of the people here.

A year later, Ngistie talked about Tuklebab during an interview with a relief worker. Holding back tears, she said through the interpreter, "There was so much suffering. All the people beg to return. We have very great problem of lack of food. There is not enough water. So many people died. We don't know the name of that place, but we call it 'The Cemetery.' Also the sun is very hot. We are not used to the heat. All the people who died were from starvation. Oooh! So many people died. Too many people died."

IV. Background

Throughout the ages in Ethiopia, landless peasants, or serfs, have cultivated and worked the fields receiving only one-fourth of the harvests. The rest went to the landowning aristocracy, local nobility, and clergy.

Ras Tafari Mekonnen, later known as Haile Selassie, came to power as Regent in 1916 and was crowned Emperor of Ethiopia in 1930. Throughout his rule, he retained the support of the feudal lords and nobles who had held land tenure and cultivation rights for generations.

In 1943, the peasants of Tigre Province, calling themselves the Tigrean National Movement, rose up against their own nobles, destroyed several government garrisons, and took control of Makele, Tigre's capital city. Haile Selassie dismissed their calls for land reform and, with armed forces deployed from Addis Ababa, successfully put down the revolt, disarmed the Tigrean peasants, imposed heavy taxes, and reinforced governmental military occupation of Tigre.

"I know nothing of any such matter," answers the Minister of Information, and I must tell you, friend, that he wasn't far from the truth. First of all, death from hunger had existed in our Empire for hundreds of years, an everyday, natural thing, and it never occurred to anyone to make any noise about it.... So how were we to know that there was unusual hunger up north? (Excerpt from *The Emperor*, copyright ©1978 by Ryszard Kapuscinski, English translation copyright ©1983 by Ryszard Kapuscinski, reprinted by permission of Harcourt Brace Jovanovich, Inc.)

In 1973, Jonathan Dimbleby went up north to Tigre Province and filmed a documentary entitled "Ethiopia: the Unknown Famine." His report showed that the government of Haile Selassie was not only slow to respond to the crisis in the north, but had shut off communications in an attempt to conceal the emergency from the outside world.

The documentary showed the Emperor serving meat to his dogs from a silver platter and then switched to scenes of starving people lying along the roadways in Tigre Province. The government continued to export record amounts of grain, the documentary said, and had blatantly misused international relief funds. In the meantime, more than 100,000 people died, perhaps 200,000, as the result of hunger.

The political results of the Hidden Famine, as it came to be called, were widespread unrest in the affected areas and the rest of the country, students demonstrating in the streets, and disaffection within the military. On September 12, 1974, Haile Selassie was overthrown in a military coup.

> The event that hastened the confrontation between the army and the Palace was the starvation in the northern provinces.... There was a lot of grain in Ethiopia, but it had first been hidden by the rich and then thrown on the market at a doubled price, inaccessible to peasants and the poor.... On the orders of local dignitaries, the police finished off whole clans of still living human skeletons.... [The conspiring officers were motivated by] the feeling of moral shame and responsibility. [From *The Emperor*, copyright ©1978 by Ryszard Kapuscinski, English translation ©1978 by Ryszard Kapuscinski; reprinted by permission of Harcourt Brace Jovanovich, Inc.]

The leaders of the coup announced the establishment of a new political and social order to be based on Marxist principles. The new military government, or Dergue as it called itself, moved to consolidate its power by imprisoning thousands of suspected opponents, but revolutionary fever was difficult to contain. Ethnic resistance movements and political organizations were formed or resurrected throughout the country.

In Tigre, the Tigrean People's Liberation Front (TPLF) was formed in 1975 by local teachers, workers, and tradespeople. Its primary aims were stated as resistance to ethnic dominion from the Amharic government in Addis Ababa and overthrow of the local feudal aristocracy. Bitter armed conflict with other indigenous Tigrean political groups marked its first few years of existence, but by the end of 1978, the TPLF could claim the allegiance of the overwhelming majority of the peasantry of Tigre.

The new military government in Addis Ababa launched an offensive against the TPLF in mid–1975. Several subsequent campaigns in the succeeding years failed to dislodge the TPLF's authority. In 1984, though, government troops occupied the capital city of Makele, controlled the main highways, and maintained garrisons in other urban areas, the TPLF administered approximately 85 percent of the Tigrean countryside.

The Relief Society of Tigre (REST) was founded by TPLF cadres in 1978 as a humanitarian organization to fight poverty, disease, and ignorance among the Tigrean population. It is structurally independent of the TPLF, having its own budget and personnel, but it coordinates its programs closely with the relevant administrative departments of the TPLF. The Relief Society has made significant progress in reducing illiteracy, especially among Tigrean women. It has established a network of health clinics and has initiated projects for soil and water conservation and for agricultural improvements.

The combination of traditional U.S. support for Haile Selassie and inflammatory Marxist rhetoric from the new government in Addis Ababa strained the relationship between the United States and the Dergue from the start. President Jimmy Carter, denouncing the continued imprisonment of thousands of students, suspended arms shipments to Ethiopia in early 1976.

Somalia, Ethiopia's eastern neighbor, emboldened by the Dergue's apparent difficulty in maintaining internal order, attacked the long-disputed Ogaden border region in 1976. Ethiopia, now unable to secure weaponry from the United States, turned to the Soviet Union and Cuba for help. The Somalis were turned back, the Dergue emerged stronger than ever, and the United States lost whatever influence it had with Ethiopia's new rulers.

After a series of power struggles within the Dergue, Lieutenant Colonel Mengistu Haile Mariam came out as the dominant figure and military dictator of Ethiopia.

... [Mengistu] inherited severe economic and developmental problems, continuing hunger in the provinces, guerrilla warfare in Tigre and Eritrea ... and continuing tensions ... with Somalia.
    ...Mengistu did not keep silent about drought and starvation in Ethiopia. In June 1978 ... Ethiopian state-controlled radio broadcast an alert that ... its northern provinces ... faced starvation....
    By November 1978 ... the Ethiopian Relief and Rehabilitation Commission issued [another] alert for international food aid....
[Better harvests over the next couple of years diminished the problem, but] again in 1982 ... late rains and large losses of sorghum and other crops caused serious food shortages.... In September and again in October, the Relief and Rehabilitation Commission issued alerts. [Jack Shepherd, "Ethiopia's Famine: The Politics of Food Aid," *Africa Report* 30 no. 2 (March/April 1985). Copyright ©1984, 1985 by the African-American Institute. Reprinted by permission of *Africa Report*.]

The Relief Society of Tigre issued its own appeals:

A severe drought in Ethiopia's northern Tigre region threatens to push thousands of impoverished peasants into neighboring Sudan as refugees.... Food supplies are perilously low. Grain stocks are falling short of the population's needs, and new supplies of grain are urgently needed if an exodus of Tigrean refugees into the Sudan is to be prevented.... REST is launching an urgent appeal to governmental and non-governmental agencies, humanitarian organizations, and individuals to support the ongoing relief efforts in Tigre. Donations of food, clothing, medicine, or cash are desperately needed.... [REST press release, January 1983.]

This and subsequent pleas from REST were largely ignored by the international community. In the eyes of international agencies, REST was only a branch of the TPLF. Efforts of support for REST would be considered support for the TPLF, and no relief organization would want to be seen as aiding the cause of a little-known guerrilla group.
    Who was to say that REST was not fund raising for the TPLF? If money or medicines were given to REST, who was to say that the money wouldn't go to buy weapons and the medicines wouldn't be reserved for the guerrilla fighters? If aid was needed in Tigre Province, better to send it through the Ethiopian government rather than through this rebel group. No matter how unsavory the Ethiopian government, it was the only channel through which international

organizations could provide aid legitimately. In the eyes of international agencies, then, the activities of the TPLF could only be seen as a hindrance to distribution of aid through proper channels.

Reports on the situation from independent sources inside Tigre were scarce and conflicting. Western officials in key positions were skeptical of REST representatives who were thought to exaggerate, even to fabricate, stories to solicit support. The REST had been warning of famine and refugees coming into the Sudan since 1978, and nothing had come of it. Peter Parr, representative of the United Nations High Commission for Refugees (UNHCR) in the Sudan's Eastern Region, stated that on the basis of information available to him,

> "I would not say there is a terrible drought, certainly not enough to generate tens of thousands coming over" [David B. Ottaway, *The Washington Post*, 18 March 1983].

Yet migration within Tigre and across the Sudanese border was occurring in the winter of 1982–83. Jon Bennet, of Britain's Durham University, spent that winter in Tigre and reported that

> ...about 250 families per day were migrating from the most affected areas in the northeast and the south towards the west where there is still some food. Some 2,000 peasants had crossed into Sudan. [Ottaway, *Washington Post.*]

The rains failed again in 1983, and the rate of spontaneous migration of refugees into the Sudan increased. Even at this late date, representatives of UNHCR continued to debate their proper role. The representative of UNHCR in Khartoum, Robert Muller, held that because the Tigreans coming across the border were coming for economic reasons instead of fleeing from war or politics, they could not be technically classified as "refugees" and were therefore not the concern of his office.

In the meantime, fighting continued. In April 1983, TPLF fighters overran the government feeding center at Korem, a village in southern Tigre. The guerrillas took 10 foreign aid workers hostage, including an American priest, and European employees of Concern and Save the Children, U.K. The taking hostage of Western relief workers was a dismaying tactic of the TPLF that would be repeated 18 months later:

...Guerrillas of the TPLF ... seized the town of Lalibela on October 19, taking 10 Westerners prisoner. The rebels later left the town, but are still holding three of the Westerners with the declared aim of showing them rebel-controlled areas that have not received famine relief aid. [Agence France-Presse, 17 November 1984.]

In March 1984, the Ethiopian Relief and Rehabilitation Commission again issued an appeal for international famine relief and warned that the rain and crop failure would lead to a "disaster of considerable magnitude" if donors did not come to the rescue.

On May 11, Dowit Wolde Giorgis, head of the Relief and Rehabilitation Commission, made a dramatic appeal for help in a speech before the United Nations Security Council.

The rains failed again in 1984. Mass starvation was now a certainty.

The duration of this drought — now in its third year — makes it one of the most severe in modern history....

Famine entails much more than the agonizing pain of physical hunger. Crop failure and the resulting loss of income can force fathers to abandon their families and seek (often non-existent) work in urban areas. Women and children, who are most vulnerable to the debilitating effects of malnutrition, are left with nothing save the seeds for next year's crops. But the seeds are often eaten when food is unavailable. In some cases, single mothers who have already lost some of their children must seek food in strange towns. They travel for days with little idea of where they will get their next meal.... Numbers fail to reveal the emotional strain on a family or describe the pain in parents' eyes as they watch their children suffer. [Kenneth Hackett, "Will the Tragedy Be Repeated?" *Africa Report* **29** no. 4 (July/August 1984).]

The United States monitored the situation in Ethiopia, but failed to take timely action:

In 1982 ... an interagency task force was set up to deal with the problem — with representatives from the State, Defense, and Agricultural Departments, together with the Agency for International Development, the CIA, and the National Security Council (NSC).

By 1983 the committee was meeting at least once a month ... and the NSC man on the committee, Fred Wettering, was one of the main obstacles to swift and massive aid by the U.S.

Refugees of the famine arrive at Fau III.

. . . The NSC man took the view that the Marxist regime in Addis
Ababa should take care of its own mess, get help from its Soviet
backers, or make strategic concessions before it received U.S.
aid.

. . . For about two years, the NSC argument carried the day, and
the massive U.S. relief effort that could have saved countless lives
never occurred. . . . [Jack Anderson, "Compassion by Committee," *Washington Post* DC9, 17 January 1985. ©1985 United
Feature Syndicate, Inc. Used by permission.]

In early 1984, the Reagan administration tied a $150 million
package of famine relief funding to a request for covert military aid
to the Contras in Nicaragua in the hope that Contra aid would be
passed on the merit of famine relief. It seems that, while criticizing
the Ethiopian government for its handling of the crisis, the United
States government itself was not above using food aid as a political

tool. In March, Senator John Danforth of Missouri freed $90 million of the famine aid, but the remainder of the emergency funds were delayed for months.

By the end of October, after NBC-TV had caused an overwhelming outpouring of public sympathy with its broadcast of dramatic footage of a BBC film showing the horrors of the famine in Ethiopia, the United States government abruptly changed its policy. Thousands of tons of food and millions of dollars of relief funds now were to be provided to the famine victims of Ethiopia; Air Force C130 cargo planes, carrying water tanks, tents, blankets, and measles vaccine, were ordered to fly to the Sudan for the Ethiopian refugees there. Still, the assistance came too late for too many.

The Ethiopian government began setting up food stations near Makele and other government-controlled towns in Tigre as early as 1982. By the autumn of 1984, these centers were inundated with starving peasants.

In 1982, Korem was a sleepy town of about 8,000 inhabitants in southern Tigre. By August 1984, the government feeding center there had become a magnet drawing in starving villagers. Fifteen thousand people had descended on the Korem feeding station where relief programs were being run by Save the Children, U.K. and Catholic Relief Services. By mid–September, the population had swollen to 30,000. On December 7 the population at Korem was estimated at between 45,000 and 55,000 with 15,000 more outside the camp awaiting entrance. Another 70,000 people had already been trucked out of Korem to resettlement centers in the previous two weeks.

Eleven feeding centers were scattered outside the town of Makele, 100 miles north of Korem. Between 50,000 and 80,000 people had converged on these feeding stations by the first week of November. Kobo, a feeding station 60 miles south of Korem holding 20,000 people, was described by one journalist as "an absolute disaster." Alamata, a feeding station situated at the foot of a mountain 12 miles south of Korem, held nearly 100,000 inhabitants by the first of November.

World Vision, the only Western relief agency at the camp, reported 90 to 100 deaths per day. Bati, a wretched camp 15 miles from Korem, held only 16,000 people, but reported a death rate of 100 people per day.

> Thousands of starving Ethiopians are pouring into the towns . . .
> and crowding along the main highways . . . to beg for food from
> passing cars and trucks. . . .
> "We're talking about an extraordinary situation where people are
> dying all over the place," a relief official says. . . . [David B. Otta-
> way, *The Washington Post*, 18 September 1984.]

At Korem, 1,549 deaths were reported in September and an estimated 1,800 in October. More than 2,500 people died there in November as a measles epidemic swept through the camp.

Though the government feeding stations assisted hundreds of thousands of starving villagers, they were inaccessible to hundreds of thousands of others in the TPLF-controlled areas. Only the International Committee of the Red Cross, the British Save the Children's Fund, and the French Médecins Sans Frontiers provided material assistance to REST overtly. Some semicovert aid from Western governments, including the United States, was provided overland through the Sudan to rebel groups, but the amounts were inadequate.

In October, the TPLF publicly called for a cease-fire to allow food aid shipments to reach Tigreans trapped by the war. Former West German chancellor Willie Brandt offered to head a commission to distribute food in the rebel-held areas. Other safe passage proposals were sponsored by humanitarian organizations from northern Europe.

The Ethiopian government dismissed all of these proposals. Acceptance would have provided the TPLF one of its key objectives: international recognition.

> Ethiopian leader Mengistu Haile Mariam told a rare news conference, "We are aware of a conspiracy from ill-intentioned people to take advantage of the drought to oblige us to make a deal with terrorists and secessionists in the north.
> "Ethiopia will never allow this to happen. We will never negotiate with the terrorists" (*Washington Post*, 17 November 1984).

Continued rebel harassment of government feeding centers only served to lend weight to Mengistu's arguments. In rejecting the proposals, however, Mengistu lost a rare opportunity to demonstrate compassion for his own people by placing humanitarian concerns above military and political considerations. The Ethiopian government discarded all pretensions to compassion on December 3 when its aircraft attacked and bombed a column of starving refugees trekking towards the Sudanese border.

With inadequate international assistance reaching TPLF-controlled areas and the situation in Tigre growing worse daily, REST began organizing to bring the first of what would eventually number more than 300,000 Tigrean refugees into the Sudan.

Some have since charged that REST used the refugees as propaganda pawns, taking them from a bad situation in Tigre into a worse situation in the Sudan in order to gain international recognition and assistance. Would not the world be moved to support REST and the TPLF at the spectacle of starving refugees being led into the Sudan?

The decision to bring the famine victims out of Tigre and into the Sudan, however, can only be explained as an act of desperation. REST estimated that between 1,000 and 1,500 people were dying daily in Tigre. According to REST member Tadella Aberaha, "The crisis had moved beyond political concerns. Our people were dying."

In the Sudan, the Office of the Commissioner for Refugees (COR) operates under the Ministry of the Interior. The COR is the Sudanese agency responsible for all refugee affairs. In September 1984, COR gave REST permission to bring refugees out of Tigre and into Sudan's Eastern Region.

It is doubtful that COR realized the extent of the migration that would shortly begin; in September 1984, perhaps even REST would have been surprised at the great numbers of people that would eventually flee under its direction to the Sudan.

The potential social and economic consequences of the migration of hundreds of thousands of starving peasants into the Sudan were enormous. The implications of so many foreigners speaking a different language and practicing radically different customs were as threatening as the tremendous drain on an already collapsing economy. The vast majority of the refugees were Christians; the Sudanese in the Eastern Region are strict, xenophobic Muslims. The political risks were so staggering that it is amazing the Sudanese allowed the Ethiopians in at all.

At any rate, the Sudanese government, citing humanitarian concerns, accepted the newly arriving Tigreans. The Sudan has a long history as a refuge for displaced peoples. Even prior to 1984, it was the country of asylum to more than 1 million refugees from wars in Zaire, Chad, Ethiopia, and Uganda. Perhaps the thought of a few thousand more Ethiopians was not particularly distressing to the government in Khartoum. Other influences to Sudanese decision makers may have been a possible desire to embarrass the Ethiopian government and the probable inability of the Sudanese army to close the border even if it wanted to. The international relief moneys directed toward the refugees would of necessity flow through Sudanese banks and circulate in part to Sudanese markets. The deciding consideration was most likely that the aid and relief moneys attracted by the refugees would provide an economic cushion that outweighed the costs, at least for the short term.

As the crisis in Ethiopia turned to tragedy and threatened to spill over in a flood of refugees into the Sudan, Western officials in Khartoum seemed oddly detached from the gravity of the situation.

As late as the summer of 1984, Jerry Weaver, the Refugee Affairs Coordinator at the United States embassy in Khartoum, continued to dismiss stories of famine in Tigre. Hunger, after all, is a fact of life in this part of Africa. Peasant peoples normally live on the very edge of starvation. The threat of famine is nothing new here. But Weaver failed to perceive that with the latest crop failure this year the threat of mass starvation was to become a reality.

Weaver was not well liked among relief agency officials who recognized his lack of acumen. In preparing his staff for a meeting with Senator Edward Kennedy, who visited the refugee camps over Christmas 1984, Ian Timm of the International Rescue Committee wrote in a memo, "Kennedy's opinion will not be the same as Jerry Weaver's, and we should not avoid describing the seriousness of the situation even if others do not think it is serious."

Weaver's cables to his superior in Washington, Richard Krieger, contradicted reports of human disaster coming from other sources.

> Months later . . . in a private meeting, face to face with Weaver at last, [Krieger] would hear the Khartoum officer admit that he had downplayed the disaster. . . . He had believed that little, if anything, could be done about the situation, and he didn't want to excite people. . . . [Claire Safran, *Secret Exodus* (Englewood Cliffs, N.J.: Prentice Hall, 1987).]

Representatives of the United Nations High Commission for Refugees in the Sudan, even though warned by REST of the impending refugee migration, failed to stockpile food and medicines. They worried that stockpiles of supplies would only attract more refugees across the border into the Sudan. Only after thousands of refugees had already begun pouring across the border, did Nicholas Morris, UNHCR's representative to the Sudan, move to procure emergency relief supplies.

In October 1984, Nicholas Morris went to Geneva for meetings to reexamine UNHCR's potential role in the drama unfolding in eastern Sudan. The discussions, which involved Richard Krieger of the United States State Department, led to the realization that the UNHCR could not stand idly by while a catastrophe occurred.

The UNHCR decided to act primarily as a channel through which the international community could contribute financial aid. It would provide funding and support services to the Sudanese COR. It would post field officers at the refugee reception centers. And it would proffer funding to private, nongovernmental agencies providing assistance to refugees in coordination with COR.

Several private voluntary agencies were already established in eastern Sudan conducting programs for Ethiopian refugees. They included Save the Children's Fund, U.K., Lalamba Association, the Joint Voluntary Agency, the International Rescue Committee, Sudan Council of Churches, SudanAid, the International Committee of the Red Cross, the League of Red Cross/Red Crescent Societies, and the International Catholic Migration Commission. These agencies assisted refugees who had come to the Sudan prior to the emergency of 1984 — people escaping the war in Eritrea Province, war and famine victims from Tigre Province, and college-age students from Addis Ababa escaping abuse and repression by communist party member peers and imprisonment and torture by the military police.

The International Rescue Committee (IRC) had been active in eastern Sudan since 1979. Its original project had been to treat and monitor tuberculosis at a refugee settlement named Tawawa which comprised mostly Tigrean and some Eritrean war refugees. Since that time, its operations had expanded to include the establishment and management of medical and public health programs in six different refugee settlements in the Eastern Region. By the end of 1983, these programs were well established and on their way to becoming self-sufficient. Throughout the first half of 1984, IRC continued to scale down its involvement and was assessing the possibility of closing its operations altogether.

In the summer and early fall of 1984, rumors of famine in Tigre were rampant in the refugee settlements. Workers for IRC noticed the appearance of scores of "new arrivals" showing up at the Tawawa settlement. So many Tigreans had migrated spontaneously into the Sudan that two new reception centers were constructed by COR at Um Rakuba and Wad el Hileau. By the end of October, Um Rakuba was home to 14,500 and Wad el Hileau to 5,000 new arrivals.

On the morning of October 31, 1984, Mike Menning, IRC/ Sudan's Country Director, received an official letter from Abdel Magid Beshir Al Ahmadi, Sudan's Commissioner for Refugees, requesting IRC to provide medical and sanitation services in three new refugee reception centers to be established about 150 miles in from the border along the Rahad Canal and Irrigation Scheme near the Sudanese town of El Fau.

The Fau reception centers would be set up to accommodate newly arriving refugees from Tigre. The medical services to be provided were to include vaccinations, supplementary feeding, inpatient facilities, and a home visitor program. Sanitation services to be provided were to include construction of latrines, control of flies and mosquitoes, water chlorination, and garbage collection.

The letter also mentioned that initial housing for the refugees would be canvas tents, and that IRC should be prepared for a population of which up to 25 percent would be in need of supplemental feeding (supplemental to standard rations to be distributed by COR). The letter left open the total population expected, but prior discussions tended to use 15,000 people (5,000 in each reception center) as a reasonable estimate.

The same day, October 31, Mike Menning and Suchat Katima (IRC/Sudan Operations Manager) met with Nicholas Morris and Ernesto Rodriguez of UNHCR. Following the meeting, Menning wrote a letter to IRC World Headquarters in New York; the following excerpts reflect his concerns and reveal some insights to the situation in the Sudan at the time:

34   Fau : An Ethiopian Famine

... There's nothing in the track record that indicates that COR
... will be able to get [food] to the new sites before the arrival of
the refugees. Nicholas Morris says that he's working on that. . . .

Besides concerns about the refugees having something to eat,
there's also the concern that there are no small number of internal
refugees. . . . We may have some very ugly incidents between na-
tionals and refugees. . . . There have already been some incidents
between nomads and farmers over grazing and fodder. . . . It
could make our job impossible if there's a general breakdown in
the social order, which isn't that far-fetched. . . .

... Once the feeding centers get underway, there's no guarantee
of its continual and reliable delivery. With IRC doing the feeding
center . . . and the food not getting delivered for one reason or
another, we could look pretty inept, if not culpable. It's for that
reason that I hope the State Department will come through with
some contingency funds. . . . There's just no way [Nicholas Morris
can] guarantee a food supply. All the pressure in the world is not
going to make the food come any faster through the existing
system.

I reiterated my insecurity about the assuredness of State [Depart-
ment] funds, again mostly due to the unknown influences of Jerry
Weaver. Nicholas Morris said he was talking to Weaver on Saturday and would take up the matter with him then. He did not want
me to talk with him first, as Weaver doesn't know that the UNHCR
is going to invite IRC to do the reception centers. In any case, Morris is looking for IRC to pay all the expatriate costs for the reception centers [— salaries, airfare, etc.; UNHCR will provide funding
for supplies and in-country expenses]. . . .

I requested that any funds from the UNHCR for the reception
centers be transferred directly to IRC. . . . My apprehension was in
knowing the problems that the Sudan Council of Churches had
experienced in Um Rakuba [refugee camp], their money having
taken a route through COR . . . and . . . not always getting to the
place it's needed on time.

Nicholas Morris mentioned that he had thought that two doctors
and four nurses might be required for each [reception center], but
then backtracked a little. . . . With sufficient local staff, I think we
can do it with one doctor and two nurses for the initial three
months. . . .

A couple of days later, Suchat Katima talked to Bob DeVecchi,
IRC's Deputy Director of Operations worldwide, in a transatlantic
telephone call that became famous among IRC staffers. DeVecchi
affirmed New York's decision to take on the new reception centers.
When Suchat voiced the same concerns that Menning had written in

his letter, especially about IRC's ability to carry out the project under present funding levels, DeVecchi, perhaps moved by NBC's broadcast a week earlier, exclaimed, "To hell with budgets! We'll get the funding, don't worry. That's not your concern. To hell with budgets! We've got to help those people!"

Where other agencies may have hesitated in such a volatile situation, IRC made the commitment. DeVecchi's courage and volition allowed the initiation of programs that eventually saved the lives of tens of thousands of refugees. It was IRC's finest hour.

V. Tuklebab

Babies too weak, too hungry to bawl make a sort of mewing cry, a pathetic plaint that reverberates through all of drought-afflicted black Africa.

That thin wail of misery and starvation echoes through the makeshift refugee camp called Tuklebab.

No roads lead here. Indeed, until a week ago, Tuklebab didn't even exist except as a nameless patch of thornbrush located about 15 miles northeast of the Sudanese town of Kassala.

Seven days later, more than 3,000 refugees from Ethiopia's war- and famine-wracked northern provinces have made camp here. Most of them are women and children. Almost all of the children — and many of the adults — are severely malnourished. Some are dying; some have died.

Meanwhile, about 450 new arrivals stagger into Tuklebab each day.

...Already the situation in the overflowing refugee camps on the Sudanese side of the border is shifting from crisis to catastrophe.

At Tuklebab, the refugees huddle in the meager shade cast by stunted thorntrees. There is no other shelter — no huts, no tents, only a single canvas canopy to protect the sickest children from the ferocious desert heat.

Lamlam Tsagi, a widow at the age of 16, grabs a reporter's hand and clasps it to her shriveled breasts. She evidently takes him for a doctor. She can no longer give milk, she says, and her baby is dying, starving.

The infant ... is 6 months old and weighs only little more than 9 pounds. His belly is puffed with hunger, an all too common sight in sub-Saharan Africa, and his arms and legs are stick-thin.

It took Tsagi 11 days to walk here from her home in Tigre, where her husband was killed in the seemingly endless war between secessionist rebels and the central government.

37

Speaking through an interpreter, she said, "Back in the village, everyone is hungry. The animals die, the people die. There is no reason to stay."

...According to Western relief agencies, between 6 and 8 million Ethiopians are on the brink of starvation. Thousands have already died.

But while the world's attention has been focused on Ethiopia itself, another human disaster is taking form virtually unnoticed in the overflowing refugee camps of eastern Sudan [Colin Nickerson, *The Boston Globe*, 17 November 1984. Reprinted courtesy of *The Boston Globe*. The placename was spelled "Tukalababa" in the original.]

About 47,000 people fleeing famine in Ethiopia have arrived in drought-stricken parts of eastern Sudan in the past 4 weeks, and 50,000 more are reported on the march.... The food situation in eastern Sudan [is] critical, and UNHCR expects no fresh supplies until the end of January [*Christian Science Monitor*, 5 December 1984].

...An outbreak of measles threatens thousands of Ethiopians scattered over a 3 mile stretch of barren desert at the edge of Tuklebab Mesa.

...The massive flow of newly arriving refugees is swamping efforts of the UNHCR and the Sudanese COR to care for them. At the Tuklebab Mesa refugee area, there are more than 35,000 Ethiopian refugees with no water or shelter and little food....

Some 3,000 Ethiopians are arriving in the Sudan each day... [*Washington Post*, 23 December 1984; Spelled "Tukulabab" Mesa in the original.]

"I'm just afraid that people walking out of Ethiopia are walking into another hell," sighed a representative of a relief agency after a visit to the Ethiopian refugee camps scattered throughout eastern Sudan....

Mass migrations to Sudan from Ethiopia started late last summer, as the fighting escalated and famine tightened its grip on the embattled provinces of Tigre and Eritrea. The Relief Society of Tigre [REST] and the Eritrean Relief Association—humanitarian wings of the antigovernment forces fighting in those areas—began organizing entire communities for the 1- to 3-month trek to the Sudan. Others have been coming on their own, and the International Committee of the Red Cross is trying to distribute food along the way.

[But the refugees] are quickly finding that Sudan is not the promised land.

Remnants of a rainless era line the one highway from Khartoum through eastern Sudan: carcasses of camels and cows, bare hills furrowed by the beds of dried-up streams, herds of goats grazing on acres of dust. . . .

Two new Tigrean settlements, Tuklebab and Wad Kowli, ran out of food on December 23rd. Some 60,000 people went hungry and another 6000 had to be held up at the Ethiopian border because there was nothing to give them. . . . Though some emergency shipments of wheat flour are now getting through, refugees throughout the east are receiving reduced rations equivalent to only 1300 calories per day.

Lack of water is another serious problem, especially at Tuklebab where there is no ground water at all. Drinking water is trucked in from Kassala, some 15 miles to the west. But a shortage of tanker trucks, fuel, and storage tanks makes regular delivery impossible. On average, each person in the camp is getting 2 to 4 quarts per day, far short of the 4 gallons per day that is recommended for refugee emergency. . . .

Shelter and clothing are nearly non-existent. . . . At Tuklebab some 34,000 people are huddled into a rocky hillside under acacia bushes — some draped with banana leaves and goatskins for added protection. Many children have no clothes; everyone else is in rags at best. Medical officers estimate that between 60 and 70 people are dying in the camp each day . . . [George Stephenopoulos, *Christian Science Monitor*, 1 January 1985. ©1985 The Christian Science Publishing Society; all rights reserved. "Tekl el Bab" in the original.]

At first sight, it is hard to believe that 20,000 human beings have sought refuge in this barren frontier region of baking sands and desolate mountains.

But then you see them, in growing numbers, the victims of famine and war in Ethiopia.

Groups of men, women, and children crouch or lie under the paltry shade of palm leaf mats and pieces of canvas strung out over the flat-topped thorn bushes. Others have crept among the boulders and niches of a "jebel" — a 1000-foot-high outcrop of desert rock, in an attempt to ward off the fierce midday sun.

As you move past the wood fires with women preparing bread or boiling lentils from their meager rations, you are followed by the plaintive wailing of hungry, often sick children. Two men help carry a young woman, too weak to walk. A stony graveyard stands nearby. . . .

The Tuklebab camp is being dismantled as quickly as possible by relief officials because of its poor location. Water must be trucked in and is limited to 2 or 3 liters per day per person, hardly enough to cook or drink. More than 10,000 of its original 30,000 squatters have been transferred to better quarters near El Fau, some 180 miles from the Ethiopian border and one of half a dozen reception centers set up by the Sudanese government ... [Edward Girardet, *Christian Science Monitor*, 15 January 1985. ©1985 The Christian Science Publishing Society; all rights reserved.]

The Great Famine affected other areas of Ethiopia, the Sudan, and other countries of the African Sahel, but it hurled its greatest cruelties into Tigre Province where rains and their accompanying harvests failed for three straight years, 1982, 1983, and 1984.

Drought and famine victims had been trickling across the border from Tigre into eastern Sudan since as early as 1982, but the period now referred to as "The Emergency" began only after the third failure of the rains. From October 1984 to the spring of 1985, more than 300,000 Tigreans fleeing from famine were organized and directed by REST into the Sudan in search of food. The first 39,000 to 41,000 people in this flood of refugees were led through the malaria-infested lowlands of western Tigre, up into the southwest corner of Eritrea, across the border 13 miles northeast of the Sudanese town of Kassala, to an area of desert wind and dust called Tuklebab.

Tuklebab. Other places presented similar horrors—Wad Kowli and Wad Sharife refugee camps in the Sudan, Korem and the other feeding stations and the devastated villages in northern Ethiopia—but only Tuklebab was known as "The Cemetery."

It is difficult to obtain much information about Tuklebab. The refugees who lived there don't like to talk about it—it's too painful for them to recall. Sudanese authorities don't like to talk about it—they are embarrassed by what happened there. REST officials don't like to talk about it—they are afraid their organization might be blamed for it. The few Westerners with first-hand knowledge of the place don't like to talk about it—they are still appalled by it.

In the September discussions, COR allowed REST to bring the famine-fleeing refugees into the Eastern Region, but not into the strategic border town of Kassala, for two reasons.

In the first place, Kassala for more than 15 years had been the reception site of a steady stream of war refugees from Ethiopia's adjacent Eritrea Province. The influx from Eritrea and Tigre increased dramatically starting with the drought of 1982. Local Sudanese already felt that the town was becoming more Ethiopian than

Sudanese, and resentment was growing. Given such circumstances, COR could not approve a massive, organized migration of more Ethiopians into Kassala. Their policy was to keep the new refugees segregated and away from the towns.

The second reason was that although the Sudanese government refused to acknowledge so until several months later, Sudan's Eastern Region itself had passed over the brink into famine. There was not enough food in Kassala to feed its own population. Had COR allowed tens of thousands of starving refugees into Kassala, the result might have been social and economic ruin and the devastation of the town.

Besides these reasons, COR was simultaneously deflecting another mass migration directed towards Kassala from famine-stricken Eritrea Province. Only a few miles away from Tuklebab, a camp named Wad Sharife was established that eventually grew to accommodate more than 100,000 Eritreans.

The COR had no choice but to instruct REST to establish camps well away from the towns. Later, these outlying locations would prove to be a major hindrance to relief efforts. In the Sudan, with shortages of vehicles and shortages of fuel, 13 miles across a roadless sand desert is formidable, even fatal.

Outside of the towns, especially after three years of drought, the only available land was, at very best, semi-desert. The REST officials, accompanied by COR authorities, decided on a site near the side of a rocky hill with no vegetation other than a few acacia thornbushes. To the north and the east, more hills of black rock protruded at curious angles from the desert floor; to the west and south, a vast expanse of flat, brown, wind-blown soil stretched to an interminable, arcing horizon. In such a forbidding area, one site would have been as good, or as bad, as another.

In selecting the site, both COR and REST failed to consider the importance of the accessibility to water. The site at Tuklebab Mesa held no groundwater for wells; the few streams that once trickled through the area had long since dried to dust. The COR assured REST that tanker trucks coming from Kassala could make sufficient water deliveries. The COR provided one tanker truck for the operation; REST furnished two more. Both COR and REST must have been dreaming to think the water situation could be managed in this way for long. Shortages of fuel in Kassala led to a restriction on the number of water deliveries;

mechanical breakdowns often prevented the trucks from running at all.

The COR officials later defended the water distribution scheme by saying it was conceived to serve only a few thousand refugees for a short duration. But as the population of Tuklebab swelled from 1,000 to 3,000 to 10,000 to 40,000, the tanker system proved grossly inadequate. People literally died of thirst.

At Tuklebab, more people died of dehydration than of starvation. Médecins Sans Frontiers, a French relief agency, rushed into Tuklebab at the request of COR, but found their medical assistance to be of little use when the basic problem remained lack of food and water. One MSF doctor noted that the human body can survive for weeks without food, but succumbs in a day or two without water in Sudan's climate. Various sources report that two to four liters of water were provided per person per day, but these are presumably averaged statistics. The refugees tell of several instances when there was no water to drink at all.

Over Christmas 1984, food supplies for the refugees in eastern Sudan were depleted. Some refugees who lived at Tuklebab say the camp was without food for only two days; others say five days passed before fresh supplies were brought in. There is no doubt, however, that many of the people who died at this time died as a result of UNHCR's failure to stockpile food months earlier before the refugees poured across the border.

The severely malnourished peasants arriving at Tuklebab were susceptible to all sorts of diseases that normally would be fought off by the body's immune system. The higher susceptibility of malnourished individuals to tuberculosis is well documented in medical textbooks. TB spread rapidly at Tuklebab.

Measles rampaged through the camp in the winter, killing untold numbers of children. Pneumonia was common in both adults and children as was typhoid. Some Western doctors estimated that up to half of the population suffered from malaria, contracted most likely in the lowlands of western Tigre and Eritrea during the journey to the Sudan.

Prolapsed rectums in children were sickeningly common. Beriberi and scurvy were not uncommon. Blindness from vitamin A deficiency was frequently encountered. Simple falls resulted in broken legs—bones were brittle from lack of calcium and vitamins.

Diarrhea-producing intestinal parasites, along with simple bacterial diarrhea, were the biggest killers of all—diarrhea, lack of water, 120°F heat, and blasts of desert winds combined to dehydrate their victims with frightening speed. Hundreds of hungry children developed diarrhea for a few hours, vomited a couple of times, and then went into convulsions and died. The graveyard at Tuklebab was the camp's most distinctive feature.

In the mornings at Tuklebab, the refugees awoke half-buried in the sand and dust that blew during the night. The dead were carried out to the graveyard in an early morning ritual. Days were spent fighting the soft, dull ache of hunger and the desperate, piercing agony of thirst. Women watched their children die. Men watched their women mourn. The only sound was the interminable coughing of those who were dying. The entire spectacle seemed as though it had been conjured by some demon as a vision out of hell.

Médecins Sans Frontiers did not even try to establish a medical records system; no statistics such as mortality rates were ever monitored. Estimates of the number of people who died at Tuklebab in the four months of its existence are guesses at best. Figures offered vary from 2,000 to 8,000, but the numbers don't begin to tell the story of what happened here. That story is told in silence by the refugees; they wear it on their faces and in their eyes.

VI. Fau : The Beginning

Tuklebab had been in existence only a couple of weeks when it became apparent that a more suitable site, with a more dependable water supply, would have to be found. The IRC had already committed themselves to attend three new reception centers to be constructed near El Fau town next to the Rahad irrigation canal. By mid-November, COR decided to close down Tuklebab altogether and move those refugees to the new El Fau reception center sites.

Preparations began immediately, but such an operation requires time to put together. Suchat Katima drove out to El Fau town with the COR authorities to help find suitable sites for the camps. They turned south from El Fau and followed the canal. They stopped at 15- to 20-mile intervals and drove stakes into the ground. These would be the future Fau I, Fau II, and Fau III refugee camps.

Mike Menning spent long hours in COR offices negotiating organizational responsibilties for food distribution, drinking water provision, and medical and sanitation services. With the help of UNHCR, Menning also made arrangements for transportation vehicles and a dependable fuel supply.

Supplies of medicines needed to be imported; local supplies would be purchased when available in sufficient quantities, and the supply procurement system already in place needed to be greatly expanded.

Besides emergency meetings with COR and UNHCR, communications were maintained with the Refugee Affairs Office of the United States embassy, and the latest developments were speedily dispatched to IRC headquarters in New York.

Sign marking the site of the Fau III refugee camp.

Ed Mangini, one of the IRC staff members, went to Tuklebab in the third week of November. To walk into a refugee camp, spend a few hours, and prepare a needs assessment is no easy task. The sick and the dying do not put themselves out on display. And the situation at this time was extremely fluid: several hundreds of new refugees were arriving at Tuklebab every day. Yet Ed recognized the seriousness of the circumstances at hand — shortages of water, a scarcity of food, few medicines, and a lack of organization in the relief effort. He reported that the refugees constituted a very ill population, suffering from malnutrition and dehydration. He listed their major medical problems as diarrheal illnesses, intestinal parasites, febrile diseases, and malaria.

The IRC/New York began recruiting for doctors and nurses. Despite Ed Mangini's grim report, Mike Menning continued to believe that, with the help of locally trained staff, three doctors and six nurses could handle the acute care needs of the Tuklebab refugees.

Even into December, COR kept repeating to Menning that "probably no more than 15,000 refugees" would be transferred to the Fau sites. No one, not even COR, could know that the population of Tuklebab would eventually approach 40,000 people. Although COR had decided to shut down the Tuklebab reception area, thousands of refugees were already making their way to the site; by early December, up to 2,000 new refugees were arriving at Tuklebab every day. Not until mid–December was REST able to divert the flood of refugees to a new migration route farther south.

No one, moreover, could have predicted the progressive and rapid deterioration of the health of Tuklebab's population. Using November's data, COR continued to report to Menning that about 25 percent of Tuklebab's population was in need of supplemental feeding; in December, the truth was that almost the entire population was near starvation. A measles epidemic broke out in early December that decimated the children, but status reports from COR to IRC were vague and infrequent.

In retrospect, the need for professional personnel was far greater than anyone in IRC had anticipated. From the information available to the IRC field office at the time, however, the plan to staff three doctors and six nurses at Fau was a reasonable decision.

But even in January and February, after the transfer of refugees from Tuklebab to Fau and after the urgency of the situation should have been obvious, Ian Timm, who replaced Mike Menning as IRC's Country Director in late December, only gradually came to recognize the critical need for more professional staff at Fau.

IRC/New York telephoned Dr. Peter Krewet in early January. He told New York that he could be ready to fly to the Sudan in a matter of days, but based on staffing requests from the Country Director, IRC did not fly him out until late March. Other personnel who could have gone to the Sudan sooner were not sent until later.

Field reports from IRC workers already at Fau always included desperate pleas for more help. The UNHCR, noting the extremely high mortality rates, also pressed for increased staffing, especially among public health and sanitation workers. As a result, Mr. Timm slowly increased his personnel roster so that by May of 1985, 45 IRC doctors, nurses, sanitarians, nutritionists, and logisticians staffed the Fau refugee camps full time. But the need for these people was in December and January, not May.

Dr. Rob Frey joined the IRC team at the end of November. He had been recruited several weeks earlier, before Tuklebab had ever come into existence, at the time when IRC's programs in the Sudan were small and growing smaller. Now he was thrown into the preparations for a massive emergency relief operation at Fau.

Dr. Frey was to be IRC's Medical Director in charge of the relief operations at Fau. Two other doctors, a nurse, a public health nurse, a nutritionist, and a sanitarian arrived during the first two weeks of December.

The newly arriving relief workers were briefed at the IRC field headquarters in Gedaref town, a sprawling, filthy slum of concrete buildings, corrugated tin shacks, and straw huts located about a two-hour drive east of the Fau sites. They held daily meetings to plan and coordinate strategies for establishing the health programs.

All had their work cut out for them, none more so than Neil Johnson, the sanitarian. Johnson was responsible for building living quarters for the other relief workers, constructing the medical clinics and feeding centers in camp, developing a water collection, purification, and distribution scheme, and establishing a solid waste disposal system not only at one, but at all three Fau sites.

Reports of the horrors of Tuklebab had reached the relief workers in Gedaref town. Their already rushed planning sessions took on a feeling of urgency as COR officials told them that the transfer of refugees was imminent.

Three days passed, then five. There was a shortage of lorry trucks for transport, and fuel was being strictly rationed in the Sudan at the time. The COR officials promised to furnish IRC with the exact date of transfer so that final preparations could be made. A few more days passed — still no word from COR.

On December 12, a going away party was held at the IRC house in Gedaref town for Mike Menning, who was leaving IRC to go to work for UNHCR. At about half past ten at night, a representative from COR showed up at the door. The first truckload of refugees from Tuklebab had arrived at Fau about three hours earlier.

The following morning, Menning, Suchat Katima, Dr. Frey, and the others piled into the Toyota Landcruiser for the two-hour trip to Fau I reception center. There they found plenty of work to be done. Failure of COR to give notice left the relief workers in a position of catching up from the start.

Approximately 650 refugees had arrived during the night, riding on the open backs of 13 lorry trucks. The journey from Tuklebab had taken about 5½ hours. Upon arrival, they had been loaded and assigned, 8 to 10 people together, to round canvas tents 10 to 12 feet across in diameter. Tent assignment by COR was based on finishing the job as quickly as possible; as a result, many families were separated, and total strangers were thrown together.

The long journey and the cold night had passed with difficulty. Food, water, and blankets were not distributed until morning. The refugees had huddled together on the ground, sharing what blankets they did have against nighttime temperatures that dropped below 50°F and a cold wind that blew hard all night.

For lack of better building materials, a clinic/hospital made of translucent white plastic sheets stretched over plastic tubing and wooden poles had been erected. As word spread that medicines and medical help were available, the makeshift structure was quickly deluged by the sick and the suffering. The 45 inpatient hospital beds were filled in an hour.

The doctors and nurses spread straw mats and plastic sheets on the ground to accommodate others judged to be critically ill and in danger of death. With the help of REST, COR, and local IRC staff members, order was maintained even while more truckloads of refugees arrived throughout the day. The IRC staff worked well into the night using kerosene lanterns and the Landcruiser headlights for illumination.

Getting the medical, nutritional, public health, and sanitation programs established was no easy task. Circumstances bordered on chaos. Pharmacy supplies were low. Food supplies were low. Prepackaged relief supply kits designed by the World Health Organization to accommodate the needs of 30,000 people for one month were depleted in a matter of days. Drinking water from the canal was so muddy that normal chlorination procedures were ineffective. Provisions, accommodations, and organization of hundreds of Ethiopian staff trained hastily at Gedaref town and brought down to Fau required an immense administrative effort all their own. Construction of straw huts to house the relief workers was nowhere near completion: IRC doctors and nurses slept on blankets on the hard ground without even minimal shelter. Refugees wandered around the camp not knowing, or forgetting, which tents had been assigned to them. No one could describe the insanity of the first several days. No one could describe the helplessness felt by the relief workers as people

Refugees arriving by lorry from Tuklebab at Fau III, January 1985.

died all around — 20, 30, even more every day. With each passing
hour more refugees died.

.As soon as things did quiet down a little, hundreds of new
refugees, all desperately ill, would arrive on the backs of lorries from
Tuklebab. Haile Micael, one of the local IRC staff members, later
recalled, "It was a terrible time, really terrible. When the lorries
came, we would go out to help the people down because they were
too high off the ground to jump. We carried many people that were
too weak to walk. Once they lifted down a woman for me to carry,
but I saw that she was already dead. That happened several times —
that they were already dead on the lorries."

Ethiopians wrap their dead in a mummy-like shroud before
burial. With so many people dying at Fau, the supplies of cloth used
in preparing the burial shrouds quickly ran out. The COR, in an effort
to maintain the refugees' cultural dignity even in death, forbid IRC
workers to bury the dead without wrapping the bodies first and the
performance of religious ablutions. Corpses began to pile up behind
the clinic, and the clinic, with the dying on the inside and the dead

stacked up on the outside, became a charnel house. One old man was found lying next to a pile of 15 bodies on Christmas Day. He had come there to die, he said. He had seen the bodies and thought that this was where he was supposed to go to die.

Two more IRC nurses from the United States reached Fau on December 18; two more nutritionists arrived on December 30. But in the meantime, up to a thousand new refugees per day were pouring in from Tuklebab. The relief workers, who had been inundated from the start, were nearly overwhelmed. They worked 16 and even 20 hours per day. They did ask if the influx from Tuklebab couldn't be slowed down for a while; they didn't realize that Tuklebab had completely run out of food at Christmas time and that the situation there was a hundred times more desperate than at Fau.

Christmas came and went. There was an attempt at celebrations: Suchat Katima drove down from Khartoum with turkey and trimmings for the relief workers and some decorations to hang up in the clinic. The workers stayed up well past midnight, however, helping to unload lorries, distributing rehydration solution to mothers and children, and carrying the weakest on makeshift stretchers to their tents.

Late at night on Christmas Day, Barb Smith, an IRC nurse, walked to the clinic and took down the decorations — she would use the cloth the next day to prepare burial shrouds for the dead.

The lorries came at night now to spare the refugees the trial of five-and-a-half hours in the hot scorching sun and daytime temperatures exceeding 105°F. And they came night after night in an endless parade of human misery. The first few weeks blurred into one long nightmare. Barb Smith later remembered walking with a COR official through a crowd of newly arriving refugees — a hazy recollection of being handed dead babies from the women in the crowd, tears streaming down her face, the sound of wailing in her ears, and the COR official telling her that the babies couldn't be buried until the priest came and the priest wasn't coming today because he was too tired.

On January 3, after Fau I finally filled up with 8,900 people, the first of more than 14,000 refugees began arriving at Fau II. Leaving one doctor, one nurse, and the sanitarian behind at Fau I, the other nine relief workers moved on to Fau II, 15 miles away, to receive the refugees there.

On January 24, the first of 13,000 more refugees began arriving at Fau III. The IRC staff, which had been stretched to the limit at one location, now found themselves covering three locations and taking care of more than 35,000 people.

It is a credit to the IRC workers that viable relief operations were set up and maintained at all, given the desperateness of the situation and the potential for complete breakdown into total disorder. Jane Swan, the public health nurse, persuaded COR to number all the tents, and she also started the process whereby all the refugees eventually carried a card upon which was recorded their health histories. Neil Johnson, the sanitarian, determined by trial and error the optimal chlorination methods with which to treat the turbid drinking water coming from the Rahad Canal. The original pole and straw structures for the feeding centers were torn down, and new structures, 10 times larger, were erected.

Dr. Simon Mardel, realizing that many of the refugees remained unaware that medical help was available at the clinic, tried to reach the people in their tents by driving around the camp in the Landcruiser and shouting through a bullhorn, "We know you're in there. We want to help you."

Those workers who were there at the beginning — Jill Seamann, Rachel Mixer, Jane Swan, Barbara Smith, Simon Mardel, Karl and Sue Schlotterbeck, and the others — were the ones battling the heat, the deprivation, the snakes, the scorpions, the flies, the suffering and despair all around them. They were the ones who established the operations that would eventually save the lives of thousands of people.

In the end nearly 40,000 people's lives were saved at Fau. That disaster had already occurred, there is no doubt; that an even worse catastrophe was averted is equally beyond question.

In December of 1984 and January of 1985, however, the situation was still desperate and grew worse daily. The elderly refugees fared the worst. In later months, newly arriving relief workers noticed that there were very few old people in camp. When they asked why, they were told simply that all the old people had died.

A letter from Ian Timm to IRC headquarters in New York, written around Christmas time 1984, details the overall situation and reveals the desperateness of the times:

...Eastern Sudan is becoming a very serious emergency with lots of people dying because of no water and no food.... The food and water shortages are expected to worsen during the next two months. There is nowhere near enough foreign nurses, doctors, or public health workers to respond to the medical needs....

IRC is the largest medical relief agency at present, and because we have the most expatriate staff, we receive informal requests to send our personnel to camps where there are thousands of people with no medical care at all. If you hear or see any reports that things are under control, these reports are not true....

[The Sudanese government and UNHCR have designated] three sites near the Rahad Canal (World Bank financed) as reception centers and to move some of the newly arriving refugees to these locations.... They have asked [IRC] ... to provide the services at these three reception centers.... At the time of conceiving the above plan, the most serious problem was 15,000 new arrivals at Tuklebab reception center which had almost no water and a limited ability to truck in water. The Fau I, II, and III sites were planned to receive these 15,000 people. After the plan was initiated, the influx continued and Tuklebab is now reported to have 31,000 residents and 7,000 more waiting outside. Also a number of other sites began to appear ranging in size from 5,000 to 25,000....

The number of agencies currently working in the Sudan are limited and their staffing levels are inadequate to deal with the magnitude of the emerging problem. At the moment IRC is the best organized and staffed.... All reports I have heard indicate that things are probably medically out of control at all the other border camps except Wad El Hileau....

The situation in the [Fau] reception centers is entirely different. When the lorries roll in with people, our doctors and nurses look through the unconscious ones to see which ones to admit to the inpatient [shelters]. There seems to be an unlimited need for oral rehydration fluid, IV fluid, and Chloroquin [for the treatment of malaria]. People arrive in rags which are not strong enough to survive a washing, and they are covered with lice.... Tents and huts are being set up frantically but never in time for the continuous flow of refugees.... The expatriate workers are working well past midnight attending to the needs of all the arrivals. The death rate at Fau I has been estimated at between five and ten [per] 10,000 population per DAY....

...People are being hauled by lorries to Fau faster than our staff would prefer, but these movements will continue because this transfer ... offers the best opportunity for [the refugees'] survival. The current estimate is that each of the three Fau sites will hold 10,000 refugees. After they each have 10,000, there will still

> be thousands at Tuklebab, not to mention all the other new border
> sites. Tuklebab is being emptied . . . because it has no water and
> because officials are afraid that continued trucking of water would
> dry out the Kassala wells, and there is no contingency plan for
> Kassala should it run out of water. . . .

The Fau sites had been chosen solely because of their proximity
to water, and the disaster occurring at Tuklebab because of its lack
of water and food made a hastily erected and disorganized Fau inevitable. The cor had no choice but to transfer those refugees as
quickly as possible. The irc was given exactly six weeks to plan,
recruit, organize, move people, procure supplies, train local
workers, and implement a massive relief operation for more than
35,000 starving refugees. No organization could have prepared sufficiently in so short a time. For the refugees, though, Fau was still
preferable to the living hell of Tuklebab. At Fau, there was a chance
for survival; at Tuklebab, all hope was lost.

And the nightmare continued. Refugees kept arriving at Fau
until Tuklebab was completely emptied. With the final truckload
coming in to Fau III on 7 February 1985, the total refugee population
at Fau was approximately 37,000. The focus of attention was turning
to a new border camp, Wad Kowli, where water was running out for
a population of nearly 100,000 people. At the three Fau camps,
suffering, death, and despair still stalked the tents, but slowly, very
slowly, a change was occurring.

VII. January–March 1985

I arrived at Fau I on January 24, having been recruited by IRC to set up field medical laboratories for diagnosing malaria, tuberculosis, intestinal parasites and other infectious diseases.

For me, the most striking of first impressions was the quietness of the camp. No children running or laughing, little movement among the adults, no traditional greetings of "Salaam!" as I walked through the tents on the way to the straw clinic in the morning. The people sitting outside the tents or standing in small groups returned neither my waves nor my glances. Words among themselves were quiet and lost to my ears by the whistling of the wind.

Emptiness. Nothing in camp was more impressive than the awareness of what was not there. No sound. No greetings or smiles. Nothing to do. Nothing to see. No amusements. If you peeked in one of the tents you would notice that there was no bed, no blankets. At the clinic, if you jabbed one of the refugees with a needle for a blood test you would notice that there was no reaction. And if you looked in their eyes you would notice that something there was missing too. There was only emptiness.

There were no clouds in the sky. The wind blew hard all day, throwing up dust in our faces, blowing over bottles of medicine at the clinic, howling in our ears, but it never blew up a wisp of a cloud. The sky was bright and blue and the sun shone hot every day, day after day, week after week.

There was no grass, a total absence of vegetation. Not a blade of grass for as far as you could see in any direction. The ground was brown and covered with a fine, silty dust. Deep cracks reached far down below its baked, dry surface.

Everywhere there loomed the horizon. And perhaps because of the flatness of the land, the horizon appeared much nearer than it ought. And perhaps because of the shimmering of the heat waves, the horizon seemed as if it were actually moving, closing closer still. Listening to the muffled voices, batting the flies from our faces, and seeing the tiny bodies wrapped up like mummies and carried out to the graveyard, it seemed as if the horizon had caught us at last, and we were living on the very edge of existence.

On January 27, I accompanied sanitarian Neil Johnson out to Fau III where refugees were still arriving from Tuklebab. Here, the Sudanese contractors who were putting up the tents could not keep up with the incoming refugees so that several thousand people were without shelter. Many had walked down to the canal and pulled weeds and brush from the water to use for shade.

From beneath a cluster of weeds a young woman caught my attention. With a pleading look in her eyes she motioned toward her lips and whispered, "Water." I was startled to hear her use the English word and quickly gave her my canteen. When she had finished I tried to start up a conversation with her, but it was useless — she spoke no other English words and I knew no Tigrenia. When I stood up to leave she pulled at me to stay. There was a desperation in her eyes which haunted me for many months to follow.

On a day in early February, while walking to the clinic at Fau I, I was pulled aside by a teenage boy and dragged into his tent. A woman whom I presumed to be his mother was lying face down on the ground. She was breathing, but erratically. Her skin was dry and burning with fever. I looked up and saw the desperate look in the eyes of her son. I tried to pick her up, to carry her to the clinic. I was clumsy, though, and nearly dropped her. The boy tried to help me and then suddenly several men appeared out of nowhere. We all helped carry her to the clinic.

One other first impression that was quite vivid was the smell. It is ghastly to recall, but the description would be incomplete without mentioning the smell. It was the smell of sickness, and of death. A sweetish, pungent odor, it was most noticeable in the clinic and the feeding center. It smelled most strongly on the breath of the patients who were dying, but even if you stayed out of the clinic you couldn't escape it. The smell of death hung over the camp like a heavy fog.

The IRC in-country administrators were poorly prepared to carry out supply and distribution requirements and to keep up adequate communications with the relief workers in the camps. Only one vehicle circulated between the Khartoum office, the Gedaref office, the three Fau camps, and six other refugee settlements.

The driver of this lone vehicle more often than not was Freda Christie. Freda also negotiated labor contracts, administered payroll, did the purchasing, distributed supplies, did the accounting, handled all the day-to-day problems that arose, and still found time to send peanut butter and canned apricots down to the relief workers at Fau. When she left IRC in June, she was replaced by three people.

Freda kept up communications with the workers at Fau and received their requests for supplies. A search through one of her filing cabinets in the Gedaref office found the following communications displaying the frantic pace of the work at Fau in January and February:

... Please have the water tanks made quickly & ship 150 beds and tanks to Tenedba [Fau I] as soon as possible. And pumps & hoses & fittings.

We need broad spectrum pyrethrium insecticide & a couple of Hudson sprayers as soon as possible. Also need 10,000 soap — check prices & maybe bring some (500-1000) now.

Pressure lamps: can we use gasoline/benzene?

Need delousing supplies for the camp — enough for 10,000 as soon as possible. I don't know what they are, but if you can find out — then go for it.

We need tetracycline as soon as possible.

We are out of ORS!!

... Bring as much I.V. solution as you have on hand, and order more of whatever they have been ordering before.

Milk powder will come in handy as we ran out of stocks as of yesterday in Fau III & today in Fau II.

One note, hastily written on the back of an envelope, simply reads, "Bring chloroquine — as much as you can, as fast as you can."

The work was exhilarating and the rapid pace kept the workers from dwelling on the suffering that surrounded them. But there was no escape from the suffering — their work plunged them into the very worst of it. One of the doctors recalled the following:

> It was my first week at Fau III and I was overwhelmed. The desolation, the need, the lack of tools, the starvation, the lines of people to be seen, the disorganization, the confusion, the long hours, the long work, the sickness. . . . Reeling in circles, I went from inpatient to outpatient to feeding center to inpatient.
>
> There was a child, 9 months old; he had been in the hospital for 2 weeks, starting to feed again. Still scrawny and malnourished, he now grabbed his mother's breast and took milk from a cup. We sent him to the feeding center. 2 days later, Sue asked me to look at him. Fever, she said; fever, I echoed. Listening, looking, no obvious source. Malaria, I said. chloroquine syrup. He vomited. chloroquine syrup. He vomited again. . . .
>
> To the hospital. I do not remember the dosage of the chloroquine injection. I am too tired to stand and am not thinking. I call to Jill, what is the dose? She hollers back and I order the injection. Do I hear?
>
> 10 minutes later and the child is grey. 15 minutes after that, despite adrenalin and cardiovascular massage and puffing into his mouth and frantic prayers — oh God, do not let him die, do not let him die — he is dead.
>
> His eyes are closed, his hands and feet tied together. He is wrapped in a shroud. His mother wails, disbelieving. Others come and hold her. Jill holds her, crying. I am stunned, sick.
>
> His body, so tiny in the shroud, is carried to the burial grounds outside camp. . . . It joins the scores of other mounds. . . .
>
> . . . I see in my mind, this baby, this mother's child, and I know, suddenly, that I gave this small one too much chloroquine, 10 times too much chloroquine.
>
> . . . His mother comes to work at the feeding center, and with gentle skill and patience, encourages other mothers to feed their wasted little ones.
>
> I return to work, treat pneumonias, treat starvation, treat malaria, even order chloroquine injections.
>
> I see his face often. His mother smiles at me, hugs me. . . .

The cor distributed food rations every 10 days or whenever food supplies came through. The rations comprised less than one pound per day per person of grains (sorghum or wheat). Oil, sugar, and beans were distributed in whatever quantities became available. No onions, no spices, not even salt for flavoring; these were survival rations, and meager at that.

Karl and Sue Schlotterbeck arrived at Fau II on January 2 to set up the supplemental feeding programs along with Diane Bianco who had arrived earlier. They quickly realized that many of the people, especially the children, were in imminent danger of starvation. Many of the children had reached the point where they wouldn't take food even when it was offered. For these children, Karl and Sue devised a therapeutic feeding program involving much more intensive feeding efforts than the supplementary feeding program. As a last resort, Karl and Sue placed plastic tubes down the noses of the smallest children through which liquid nourishment could be delivered.

Feedings consisted of high-calorie wafer cookies and a porridge made from sorghum, sugar, oil, and milk. Along with the regular food rations to the camp population, these supplemental feedings saved the lives of thousands of children.

At the end of January, more than 2,800 children were enrolled in the supplemental feeding program, and 1,100 in the therapeutic program. Classification as a supplemental or therapeutic feeder was based on recorded heights and weights. People who weighed less than 70 percent of the expected weight for their height were placed in the therapeutic feeding program; those whose weights fell between 70 percent and 80 percent of the expected level were placed in the supplemental feeding program; those who weighed more than 80 percent of their normal weight based on height received only the CoR-supplied camp rations.

The food provided to the supplemental and therapeutic feeding programs came through the World Food Program and, later, CARE. A significant amount was donated by OXFAM, a British agency, and most of the powdered milk originated from the United States.

More than once, food supplies ran out. One night in late January at Fau I, the relief workers were awakened well after midnight by a lorry truck carrying 150 fifty-pound bags of powdered milk. Rather than complain about the late hour, they jumped out of bed and unloaded it enthusiastically — they had run out of milk two days earlier. According to Karl's January report,

Supplies of sugar ran out several times, so the milk was lower in calories than it should be; the milk powder supplies were also interrupted several times....

Later in the same report, Karl mentions

Numbers for January have received lower priority than getting the programs set up. [Records have been kept] in Fau II and Fau III ... but not accurately ... so rather than report inaccurate numbers, [I will say] roughly 60 percent of the children in therapeutic feeding who have been reweighed are gaining weight ... on the other hand, an unacceptably high number of children are being reported as having died.

Record keeping was attempted by all the programs, but the organization was still grossly understaffed and the workers severely overworked. In a surveillance report required by UNHCR, rather than fill in the blank spaces next to each listed disease, Rob Frey, IRC's medical program director, just scrawled across the page, "Unreliable data," and to the side, he scribbled, "Most died from malnutrition."

At night in their straw huts, by the light of candles or kerosene lanterns, the relief workers wrote letters home. Sue Schlotterbeck's letters all said the same thing: "It's very hot, too many people are dying, and we need more help."

Excerpts from letters written by other workers help paint a fuller portrait of Fau from January to March:

27 January 1985
I'm really out in the bush this time ... there are 6 of us staying in a cluster of 4 grass huts....

1 February 1985
The camp is really sad. There are about 10,000 people all living in little tents supplied by the United Nations. Every one of them is sick and malnourished. They've already set up a feeding center so nobody here starves to death. When trucks carrying food show up they usually carry enough food to last only a few days and then everyone prays that another one will show up before the supply runs out. You can imagine how much food is needed to feed 10,000 people just for a day! And there is at least a dozen other camps — most of them larger — one, Wad Kowli, has 80,000 people

Patient at the Fau I feeding center.

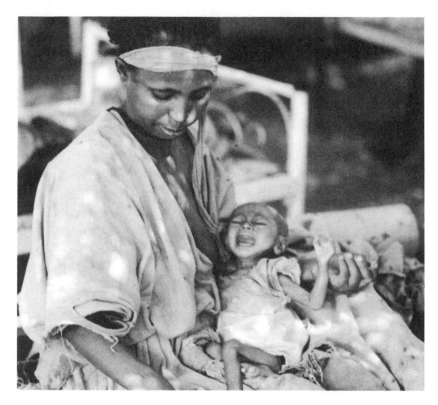

Mother and child at IRC inpatient clinic at Fau II.

and is growing by 500 new arrivals per day. Here at Fau I, the doctor thinks that ¾ of the people have malaria. One of the American workers here has malaria right now. He hasn't come out of his hut since I've been here....

It's sad to see the kids so skinny and sick. They keep the kids' heads shaved except for a tuft of hair on the top. I asked one of the people who speak English the purpose of the custom. He explained that the tiny tuft of hair is left for the angels to pull the children up to heaven when they die....

1 February 1985
...Last night 14 people died — half of them children....

6 February 1985
...The climate is a big change from home. It's hot and there's nothing to look at. For miles ... only barren ground with a few thornbushes....

6 February 1985

...In the 3 Fau camps here, there are just 14 Americans and 2 British doctors providing medical and sanitation services for more than 30,000 people. There is a big camp near the border called Wad Kowli that has about 90,000 inhabitants. They say the water supply there will dry up in 2 or 3 weeks, so they will all have to be relocated. Rumor has it that 8000 or 10,000 people will be sent to each of the 3 Fau's. God, I hope not. We're too short staffed to handle the populations we already have — 8500 at Fau I, 14,000 at Fau II, and 12,500 at Fau III....

8 February 1985

...There are thousands of flies, crawling in your hair, your ears, your eyes....

12 February 1985

...It's strange to think that I don't really see a lot of death; most of them die during the night and are carried off and buried at sunrise. The children are the most vulnerable. I've heard that more than 10 percent of all the children have already died — most before they ever reached Fau....

...Nearly 1000 refugees died at the 3 Fau's last month....

14 February 1985

...The people here at Fau II came from a place called Tuklebab and were moved here when Tuklebab ran out of food and water. The tents here were set up by UNIICR; food is distributed by COR. IRC is supplying medical and sanitation supplies and personnel....

20 February 1985

...It's difficult to describe the situation here because it's so full of contrasts and contradictions. The worst is as bad as the pictures they show on television, but the pictures on television don't show the best. For every child lying near death in the feeding center, there are 10 in the camp laughing and playing. That's not to say that life isn't hard here for everyone. When UNHCR ran out of tents, nearly 3000 people at Fau III sat in the desert for a week until any shelter at all could be provided. Flies swarm everywhere, attracted by the death....

21 February 1985

...There was a group of U.S. congressmen and senators visiting Fau III for a day last week. Had they come a week earlier, they could have seen refugees sitting on the ground with no shelter over their heads to protect them from the sun....

21 February 1985
. . . There are probably more than 2000 Ethiopians crossing the
border at various locations each day, and the flow is expected to
get larger. Sudan is not in such good shape itself. More than 1%
of its foreign currency reserves were leaving the country daily, so
the government froze all foreign currency accounts a few days ago
(don't know yet what effect that will have on our importing supplies). Yesterday a presidential decree banned the sale and purchase of all grain, flours, and lentils. Gasoline, diesel, and
kerosene are all rationed. It is certainly an interesting place to
be. . . .

22 February 1985
Tell all your friends to donate money if they can. And if they're
afraid their money won't get through or will only go to make relief
officials rich, then ask them to offer a prayer — over here we need
both.

18 March 1985
. . . Saturday . . . I should have a big truckload of supplies
waiting for me. . . . Getting supplies is proving to be my biggest
headache. . . .
. . . A good part of my day is spent just waiting around for a
vehicle to bring me back and forth between the camps. . . .
. . . But even if we had enough vehicles, that wouldn't solve the
problem. [Fuel] is just about impossible to get — and then only in
small quantities. We've only got about a 12-day supply of diesel
left. Once we run out, the trucks will stop running, and then we'll
really be in a mess. . . .

25 March 1985
. . . We had an outbreak of spinal meningitis [at Fau III], but for
once things worked out like they should. After the first 2 suspected
cases, we confirmed . . . that it was meningococcal meningitis —
very contagious and usually fatal. Then we went out and discovered that the 2 patients' tents were near to each other and we
sent off an urgent message to Khartoum for vaccines. The vaccines
arrived 3 days later (record speed for this place). By that time 2
more people had died and 7 more suspected cases admitted to the
hospital. Now everyone is vaccinated. . . . It could have been
much worse. . . . Quick action . . . prevented a disaster.

28 March 1985
I hear they had some disturbances in Khartoum yesterday over
an increase in the price of food and the devaluation of the Sudanese
pound. Things are real peaceful in Gedaref though. . . .

29 March 1985

...No electricity so I'm writing by candlelight....

...We had to evacuate the compound at Fau III because of snakes. We killed 17 [last week] and 2 people were bitten — one of the doctors nearly lost her foot....

31 March 1985

...We had some big-time journalists at Fau III before the meningitis.... One of them was a TV cameraman for NBC San Francisco, one was from the Chicago Tribune, and one was from Newsweek....

Most of the IRC people seem to despise the reporters who come. A few of them are a bit arrogant and insensitive — one photographer taking pictures in the hospital of a mother and child kept telling the mother not to smile. But I think that publicizing what is happening here is a good thing....

31 March 1985

...I'm working at a camp called Fau III, but I'm staying at Fau II compound where there are fewer snakes....

Amid all the confusion and frustrations of those first two or three months, something was happening. Doctors, nurses, nutritionists, and sanitarians were doing their work and training local people to assist them. They established life-saving health programs, and every day they struggled to improve the effort. Although it wasn't particularly evident, the refugees were gradually, slowly, beginning to regain their health. You wouldn't notice it if you spent your days at the clinic watching the sick coming, sitting, waiting to be seen, but you might notice it if you walked through the camp — women smiling and saying "Salaam," young men enthusiastically approaching to shake your hand, children playing with balls made out of rags tied together and pulling home-made toys made out of tin cans on a string. Gone were the days of silent emptiness.

Although the medical teams were at the center of visiting journalists' attention, the nutrition and the less glamorous sanitation programs had a greater impact on a greater number of people. The impact of the feeding programs is obvious; providing precious nourishment was the key to the entire effort. Less obvious, but no less important, was the sanitation program's ensuring safe, chlorinated drinking water. There were lapses: often fuel was insufficient to pump the water from the canal to the chlorination tanks, and the amount of

Boys playing with home-made toys made from wood, string, and flattened sardine cans.

chlorine to be added had to be determined on a trial and error basis and fluctuated with the turbidity of the water, but as these problems were solved and the sanitation teams gained expertise, the incidence of diarrheal diseases and intestinal parasites began to decline.

Dr. Richard W. Steketee, a consulting physician from the Center for Disease Control in Atlanta, visited the Fau camps on February 25 and 26. In his report, he criticized the emphasis on curative programs over public health and sanitation:

> Malnutrition remains a major problem and, coupled with a stable, potable water supply system, supplemental feeding for malnourished and vulnerable groups should be the major priorities for consolidating efforts. Until these problems are fully addressed, all curative/medical therapeutic efforts will be ineffective at best.

Dr. Simon Mardel recognized the importance of public health community education in the effort to improve refugee health. One evening in early March, I accompanied Dr. Mardel and some of the other Fau I workers into the camp. We had more vehicles available for use now, and we rode into camp on the back of a Toyota pick-up. We were greeted by one of our translators in an open area between section D and section E. Within seconds a crowd of refugees started to gather to see what we were up to. Within a few minutes, a throng of about 300 people had encircled us. Then Dr. Mardel did what he had come to do — deliver a lecture on the use of oral rehydration solution.

Dr. Mardel spoke out loudly and then the translator, using a bull-horn, repeated the phrases in the Tigrenia language: Oral rehydration therapy is used to treat the dehydration that accompanies severe diarrhea — and dehydration, augmented by the scorching heat and parching wind, is the leading cause of death in the camp, especially for children.

The theory is simple: dehydration kills by draining the body of salt-containing fluid. Rehydration therapy is the replacement of the salts and fluid. Foil packets of ors (Oral Rehydration Salts) were available at the irc clinic. The packets contain dextrose, sodium, potassium, and chloride salts in such quantities that, when mixed in a liter of water, will be optimally absorbed by the body. Drinking the ors will not cure the diarrhea, but it will keep the patient alive until the diarrhea is cured.

The doctor went on to explain that, even in their home villages, the refugees could prepare ors simply and cheaply by adding a handful of sugar and pinch of salt to a liter of water.

After the lecture, the refugees in the audience asked several questions. Everything had to be translated two or three times, but the kinds of questions posed displayed a remarkable understanding and a real interest in the subject of the lecture: "What do I do if my baby doesn't like the taste and refuses to drink the ors?" "How much ors can I drink in a day — can too much ors be dangerous?" "If the water is dirty, what good is the ors?"

The doctor answered these and other questions as best he could. I remember thinking to myself, "This is public health at its most basic, and most effective."

The lecture and the question and answer period lasted over an hour. During that time, several of the refugee children came up to me, tugged at my shirttail, pulled the hair on my arms, made faces, kicked me in the shins, and acted as young children are wont to behave. Only one of them was quiet, a terribly malnourished little boy whose knees and elbows seemed swollen in comparison to his arms and legs because of the shrinking away of muscle tissue. He put his arm around my waist and buried his shaved head into my side. I put my arm around his shoulder, and we stood like that for nearly the entire hour.

Once back at the living compound, the other relief workers and I sat at a wooden table by the light of two kerosene lanterns under the straw roof that served as the common dining room. The cook had prepared our dinner, the same dinner we had had for two weeks: boiled lentils served with a bread that had a funny taste from all the weevils in the flour. "I see you've met Nagassy," said Deborah Young, one of the nurses along on our evening outing, "the skinny one with his arms around you."

She then went on to relate Nagassy's story: He had been sick in Tuklebab and under the care of REST healthworkers at the time of the transfer to Fau. In the confusion of the moment, his family was not informed when he was placed on the lorry. They remained behind and had never been heard from since. When the trucks were unloaded that night, little Nagassy was overlooked and wasn't assigned a tent to live in. For two weeks he slept outside in the wind and the dust, lacking a blanket and wearing only torn rags to keep him warm during the cold nights. In the morning, hunger would awaken him gnawing at his stomach, and he would stumble from tent to tent, begging for food. The people from whom he begged had precious little to spare from their 400 grams per person per day rations. It seems no one believed him when he pleaded he didn't have a tent or a ration card to get his own food. He didn't know anyone from REST to whom he could turn for help, yet he managed somehow to survive.

One night, as usual, he lay down on the chilled ground and cried himself to sleep, but the next morning he did not wake up. He was found lying in the dust unconscious, and someone carried him to the sheet-plastic clinic for the foreign doctors to see.

Deborah looked at him and decided he was beyond hope. She had seen others like him, dozens of others, wasted away beyond the chance of recovery. Frustrated, she mechanically started a dextrose IV on him and quickly moved on to the next patient, one for whom she could do more.

Nagassy didn't die that night as expected; nor did he die the next night, nor the next. A plastic tube was threaded down his nose and into his stomach. A syringe pumped a solution of powdered milk and sugar through the tube. After several days Nagassy regained consciousness and recovered enough strength that the tube was taken out and he ate food that was prepared for him — a porridge made of corn and soy meal and sugar and milk.

He stayed in the hospital for two months even after he had recovered enough to be discharged; he still didn't have a tent to sleep in. He formed a special attachment to Deborah and followed her everywhere. "Now he goes to the feeding center twice a day," said Deborah, "and REST has found a tent for him to live in and people who'll look after him."

The next day I spied Nagassy at the hospital following Deborah around. When he saw me, he came up and put his spindly little arms around me and hugged me as hard as he could. I was carrying several passport photographs of myself in my wallet so I gave him one thinking that he might enjoy it. He was thrilled.

I made a point of walking through the camp on the way to the living compound at the end of the day rather than walking along the canal or riding in the truck. I played catch with the children along the way with their ragballs, and I let them pull the hair on my arms — a source of never-ending wonder to them. By the time I'd walked to the edge of the camp, I felt like the Pied Piper with 10, 20, even 30 children following close at my heels.

At the very last tent lived a little girl who couldn't have been more than three years old. When she saw me coming and the throng behind me, she ran toward me with her arms straight up in the air. I picked her up and lifted her over my head and then set her back down again. Then she screamed in terror and ran back to her mother's arms in front of the tent. We followed the same routine every day and gave a great laugh to anyone watching. One day I caught her before she ran away and asked her name. "Hanah," she replied in a terrified whisper and then fled back to her mother.

Mistakes were made, the number of Western relief workers too few, inadequate planning was apparent, but we made progress — tremendous progress considering the situation, terrific progress compared to the continuing tragedies in other camps. The most telling statistic was the mortality rate, a calculation of the number of people

Top: *Children who followed me during a walk through the camp at Fau I.*
Bottom: *Hanah.*

Young girl weeps on the embankment of the canal.

who died during the month based on a population of 10,000 people. More than any other indicator, the mortality rate showed the impact of the health interventions at the Fau camps. For the three Faus as a whole in January, the mortality rate was an incredible 311 deaths per 10,000 population. In February, there were 290 deaths per 10,000 population. By March, the death rate had dropped to 216 per 10,000 population. (For a discussion of these calculations and the numbers they are based on, see the Appendix.)

Although the declining mortality statistics were encouraging, death remained an all too common occurrence. From January 1 to March 31, 1985, there were 1,702 deaths recorded at Fau—in three months nearly 5 percent of the entire population had died. The deaths during the awful months at Tuklebab cannot even be estimated.

One evening in late March, I walked along the embankments of the canal to take some pictures of the sunset. I was startled to see a young refugee girl sitting by herself so far from camp. She was crying softly in the heat of the afternoon. I approached her and bent forward, but being so ignorant of the language, I remained dumb. She continued to cry soft silent tears and was either unaware of or indifferent to my presence. When I looked back, she was still there, crying silently, alone in her grief.

VIII. April–June 1985

The three Fau camps were located along the Rahad Canal which drew water from the Rahad River, a tributary of the Blue Nile. Fau I was set up only a quarter-mile away from a permanent Ethiopian refugee settlement called Tenedba that had been in existence since 1981. Across the bridge on the other side of the canal lay Sudanese Tenedba, a tiny Sudanese village of less than a thousand people, but where a small market boasted three tailor shops and stalls selling grapefruits, tomatoes, and goat meat.

Fau II was situated about 15 miles farther north on the canal, isolated in the Sudanese desert and within walking distance of nowhere. Fau III, similarly isolated, was 10 miles farther yet up the canal. The Sudanese town of El Fau was located on the main Sudanese highway about 25 miles north of Fau III. A tarmac road connected Fau II and Fau III to El Fau, but the road to Fau I was a simple trail in the dust.

All three of the camps presented rectangular layouts, the length parallel to the canal. At Fau I and Fau III, only 50 yards separated the canal from the nearer rows of tents; at Fau II, more than 200 yards lay between the camp and the canal. At the center of each camp stood the irc clinics and feeding centers. (The first makeshift clinics made of plastic sheets had been removed and replaced by wooden pole and straw structures in March.) A main road leading to the clinics ran from both sides through the center of the camps parallel to the canal. The tents were close together, especially at Fau II where only a few feet separated neighbors.

Open spaces between the tents running perpendicular to the canal divided the camp into blocks, or sections. Fau III was the longest of the camps, having sections A through G. When UNHCR's supply of canvas tents ran out, straw was obtained, and the people in sections F and G built tiny hovels for themselves no more than 5×7 feet in area, with no windows and an open space for a door, housing up to eight people.

Scorpions crawled through the camp at night. Each month several scorpion stings were brought into the clinics. Though extremely painful, the stings were not deadly. In eastern Sudan, scorpions were more of a nuisance than a danger.

Fau III was famous for its snakes — 2-foot-long vipers, African cobras, aggressive and numerous. Two refugees died at Fau III from snakebites: one an infant, the other a teenage girl who had been bitten repeatedly.

Most of the relief workers who lived at Fau came home with at least one snake story. A nurse at Fau II had been awakened one night by a snake falling from the ceiling of her straw hut onto her bed. Dr. Carol Beechy, after having been stung by a scorpion a few days earlier, was bitten by a snake in March. Though she eventually recovered, for a few days it seemed that amputation of her foot might become necessary.

My own snake story occurred at Fau III in early May. Since the moon always shone bright enough on these cloudless nights, I had acquired the habit of walking without a flashlight. Shortly after dusk, after a dinner of boiled lentils and peanut butter sandwiches, I walked across the relief workers' living compound, a rectangular enclosure of seven grass huts surrounded by a tall grass fence. At one of the huts I pulled back the mosquito netting that had been strung across the doorway to keep out flies and took a half step forward. I heard a sound, like an airy breath — "Hhhha!"

In slow motion I looked down to see a viper in the soft moonlight, inches from my foot, coiled to strike. An explosion of adrenaline and it seemed as though I bounded 50 feet through the air. "Snake!" I yelled, and the two Ethiopians who guarded the compound at night came running with a rake and a shovel — by now, this was a familiar routine for them.

But the snake was gone. Was it still inside the hut? The guards searched thoroughly with the kerosene lamp — under the bed, behind the bags of clothes, but they found no snake. Still, it could have climbed up the wall, and perhaps it now lay hiding in the thatch roof.

I remembered the story of the snake that fell from the roof onto the bed at Fau II, and I pulled my bed out of the hut, and for the rest of the summer I slept outside.

Most of the relief workers who came to work for IRC at Fau had come under 90-day contracts; a few stayed six months; very few stayed longer than that. In the months from January till June, several of the workers went home before the expiration of their contracts. Early termination was not uncommon even among the 90-day staff.

The number one reason for early termination among the relief workers was disease. Several people were sent home with serious illnesses. In a March report, Dr. David Heiden listed the illnesses that had occurred among the six expatriate staff during the month:

- Amebic dysentery and hepatitis...
- ...Diarrhea, scorpion bite, poisonous snake bite...
- Amebic dysentery
- Trachoma
- ...Episodes of diarrhea
- Bacillary dysentery

Any relief workers traveling to remote areas of the world take the chance of developing personal illnesses. At Fau, however, because of the overwork, the punishing climate, and the high incidence of infectious disease among the inhabitant population, this chance became a certainty. Everyone got sick at one time or another; that was part of the job.

In April, at Fau, it seemed as though everyone was sick all the time. Because the relief programs in camp were so understaffed, the workers put off going into Khartoum to receive medical treatment. The result was more sickness, exhaustion, and a terrible depletion of morale.

Dr. Robert Frey wrote to Ian Timm,

...Problems of logistics continue and of staff morale.... Expat staff seemed to hit a new low with 5 staff out with potentially serious ailments.... This dramatized the thin nature of our staffing, where a program often depends on a single person....

Dr. David Heiden wrote,

...Morale is definitely not ideal.... Certain aspects, heat, dust,
flies, oppressive landscape are unavoidable. The incredible level
of illness [in camp] ... coupled with chronic [supply] shortages
... adds to frustration.

Dr. Heiden concluded that,

[Illness among the relief workers] remains the most extraordinary
drain on morale—it can be minimized by better staffing and a
more humane living environment.

For some relief workers, the biggest single drain on morale was
the flies. They were incredible in January and February, but by May
and June, they had become outrageous, multiplying by billions.

In camp, whether examining patients, dispensing vaccinations,
or measuring chlorine in the water, everything had to be accomplished using only one hand—the other hand was in constant motion
chasing the flies away from nose, eyes, and mouth. They buzzed
when they got entangled in your hair and bit when they got up your
pants leg.

Even writing a letter was impossible. A dozen flies would land
on your hand and pen as you were writing. When people did write
letters home, they would beg their relatives to send them cans of
Raid.

In March and April, after a long day in camp, we sat around the
table drinking warm Pepsi and mindlessly swatted the table and
chairs with the flyswatter, trying to see who could kill the most flies
in a single swipe. In May and June, it was no longer a challenge to
kill even six or seven flies with a single stroke, and the trick became
trying to kill just one.

The air was so thick with flies that they literally died in mid-air,
dropping dead on the top of the table or against the pages of your
book if you attempted to read. I remember walking by the hut of one
of our doctors at Fau II in April. I heard a shout from the inside:
"Goddamn flies!" and then a medical textbook came sailing out the
door.

Most of us spread a mosquito net over the doors of our grass
huts in a vain attempt to keep out the flies. One day in May we

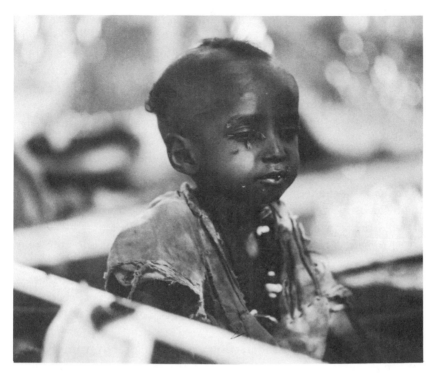

Patient at IRC inpatient clinic, Fau II, is covered by the unavoidable flies.

returned from camp to find that the wind had twisted the mosquito netting on one of the doors over on itself. Flies trying to enter the shade of the hut had gotten caught in the folds and died. We emptied out the net into a five-gallon plastic bucket and nearly filled it with dead flies.

We joked among ourselves that when a new worker arrived at Fau, if a fly fell into his tea, he would throw out the tea. After a month at Fau, he would just spoon out the fly and drink the tea. After two months at Fau, he would just drink down the tea, fly and all.

At dusk, the flies magically disappeared. We awaited every sundown, for it was only after dark that we could relax and get away from the flies. But no one slept past dawn. At the first sign of light, the flies returned in full force. They got underneath the sheets and into our ears and buzzed us maddeningly awake. Everyone greeted the new day in the same way: "Goddamn flies!" we muttered and got out of bed.

For four months, IRC's Country Director, Ian Timm, had resisted increasing the relief worker staff beyond what he felt was minimally necessary. Now with half his staff sick and the other half complaining bitterly, he moved to bring in more people. By early June there were 12 to 15 expatriate staff working at each Fau camp, and for the first time staffing was adequate to meet the needs.

By mid–May, all the workers who had been at the Faus at the beginning were gone, having completed their contracts or gone home sick. The new people coming in to replace them, not realizing the progress that had been made since December, were sometimes quick to criticize the inadequacies of the programs as they found them. But they did bring new ideas and fresh approaches, and the programs showed the improvement.

Mortality rates continued to decline. In April the rate was 90 deaths per 10,000 people per month. In May the rate was 53 deaths per 10,000 population per month. And in June the death rate dropped to 39/10,000/month. The relief programs had been successful — the death rate in June was eight times lower than the rate in January. (See Appendix.)

I still remember the satisfaction we felt at Fau II in April the first day that there were no deaths reported. We knew a milestone had been reached and we congratulated ourselves, but at the same time we couldn't help questioning our effectiveness. Couldn't we have been faster? Couldn't we have done more? But in camp a whisper circulated among the people as if carried by the wind: "No one died today."

Problems in the programs that had gone unnoticed before were discovered and resolved. One of these problems had both medical and political implications.

When the Fau camps were first established and during the first few months of their existence, the IRC field office in Gedaref town recruited Ethiopian refugees living in Gedaref and the nearby refugee settlement of Tawawa to be trained to assist in the provision of health services at Fau. More than 250 Ethiopians were recruited and sent to Fau. Because none of the refugees at Fau spoke English and none of the relief workers spoke Tigrenia, the language of Tigre, the Ethiopians sent from Gedaref and Tawawa were to act as translators as well as to assist in the physical work of the programs.

What the IRC office in Gedaref didn't realize was that by recruiting

Ethiopians who spoke English and by selecting those with the best education, they were discriminating against native Tigrenia speakers in favor of those who spoke Amharic as their first language. For demographic and political reasons inside Ethiopia, the Amharas as a group are better educated and more likely to speak English than are the Tigreans.

The two groups have been in conflict for centuries. When the Kingdom of Axum was cut off from the Red Sea by the Muslims in the early Middle Ages, the people turned inward. Indigenous people further south were assimilated, the seat of political power gradually moved southward from Axum to Gondar through a series of unceasing internecine wars among the Ethiopian city-states, and the language changed in the process.

In modern Ethiopia, the political center has been relocated still further south to Addis Ababa, and power is held by the dominant Amharic speakers. The Tigrenia speakers of Tigre and Eritrea provinces continue to resist this domination. Ethnic pride and the collective memory of ethnic bloodshed through the ages are at the root of the wars being waged in these areas today.

The IRC sent down more than 250 Amharas to work in the Fau refugee camps with Tigreans, mixing people who at best feared and distrusted each other, and at worst despised each other because of the age old conflict. To make matters worse, most of the Amharas sent to Fau as translators were unable to speak Tigrenia! With Ethiopian unemployment in Gedaref near 100 percent, when a potential job came along that required Tigrenia, the applicants simply lied and said they spoke the language.

In the camps, the doctors were often puzzled by long discussions between their translators and their patients over simple questions. They couldn't have realized that the translator and the patient were trying, often unsuccessfully, to find common words with which they could communicate.

Several months afterward, one of the translators, Yohannes Hiwot, admitted, "When I first went to Fau, I didn't understand Tigrenia language. Doctor would become upset if I took a long time. So if I didn't understand what the patient said, just I would tell the doctor 'diarrhea' or 'fever' or 'vomiting'. And if he asked for how many days, I would make that up too."

Many of the Amharas held the Tigreans in the disdain borne of generations of prejudice. One of the female Amharas who worked in the IRC Gedaref field office couldn't understand all the attention being directed to the people at Fau. "After all," she said, "they are only peasants."

Many other Amharic workers at Fau, however, sympathized with the distress and suffering of the Tigreans in camp. One of the workers who helped record weights and heights at the feeding center at Fau II told me, "The government [in Addis Ababa] did not try to keep secret the drought in Tigre. They talked about it on the radio and television, but I didn't know it could be like this."

Another Amharic worker, Abie Girma, when asked why he came to Fau to work, replied, "Because I need a job to survive. But I am happy to help these people. They are also my countrymen."

Most of the Amharic workers at Fau came because it was the only place where they could find employment. They felt no particular sense of mission, but they did try their best to perform their jobs well. Ethnic tensions were apparent at the outset, however, and over time they increased. The underlying feeling was expressed most clearly by Ashebar, the head of the REST delegation at Fau, at a meeting with IRC staff: "We appreciate the help of the IRC Amharic workers, but now they must leave to allow us to take care of ourselves."

Araya, the leading REST member at Fau III, complained further: "IRC pays Amharas to come from Gedaref to work here when there are enough Tigreans here who need the work. We will all go home in a few months. We would like IRC to hire us and to teach us and train us so we can take care of our own people when we return home."

It was apparent that the men in camp really had nothing to do. They had lost the traditional role of being the breadwinners for their families. Rations were provided and it was generally the women who stood in the long lines. The men loitered about all day with nothing to occupy themselves. Feelings of usefulness eroded along with their sense of self-worth. If they had not yet lost respect from their families, they were beginning to lose their respect for themselves. Their families were being cared for by foreigners and Amharas. Bitterness arose. Feelings of helplessness gave way to feelings of anger.

Daniel Derebe worked at Fau II as an examiner — the local equivalent of a doctor, diagnosing illnesses and prescribing treatment. He shared a tent with six other Amharic staff. While most of the Amharic workers spent their free time playing soccer or cards, Daniel stayed in the tent and painted. He produced several beautiful canvasses during his time at Fau. Gentle and kind, he, perhaps of all the Amharic workers, held the greatest compassion for the people of the camp.

In late April, Daniel was attacked in broad daylight outside the IRC clinic by several men carrying sticks and clubs. The assault was over in seconds; there were no witnesses. Whether the attackers were REST members or under the direction of REST is a matter of conjecture. Following the attack, REST offered no apologies or expressions of regret.

Daniel left Fau a few days later and is now living, unemployed, in Khartoum. He is missing several teeth now and speaks more slowly and less clearly than he used to.

Similar attacks occurred over the next few months; fortunately, they were very infrequent. That most of the Amharic workers chose to remain on reflects their desperate need for employment.

The problem was recognized by the relief workers. In a report received in early April, David Heiden wrote:

> Amharic staff continues to provide 95% of our support staff and these people continue to perform excellently . . . [but] efforts need to be made to recruit and train future health workers from the Tigre camp population. . . . [This] will contribute far more towards making the camp people self sufficient.

The issue even threatened to cause divisions among the relief workers. Some wanted to replace all the Amharas with Tigrenia speakers, the sooner the better. Others rejected the dismissal of loyal workers on the basis of ethnic discrimination.

When Dr. Rich Kovar replaced Dr. Rob Frey as IRC's medical director in June, many Amharas had already left the Faus, fearing for their personal safety. Dr. Kovar weeded out other Amharas who were not up to standard in performing their jobs or who had run afoul of REST for one reason or another. Several Amharas remained; most of those remaining were accepted by REST and the camp people, but a few still feared to enter the camp alone at night.

In retrospect, it was unavoidable for IRC to hire so many Amharas to work at Fau. People who could be trained quickly were needed immediately to work day and night in an emergency situation. How could the expatriate staff train workers who spoke no English or who were illiterate even in their own language, especially for jobs which required reading and writing and considerable technical skill such as examiner, lab technician, and pharmacist? As stated earlier, educated, English-speaking Tigreans were difficult to find; educated, English-speaking Amharas were plentiful. It is significant that REST and the camp people complained only after March, after the emergency had been contained. The Amharic workers deserved a better thanks than they received.

Still, it was recognized that REST's stance had merit. The IRC made a strong effort to hire and train workers from within the camp. The IRC also had the extraordinary success of recruiting a Tigrean physician to work at Fau and direct the training of the new health workers from the camp. Thanks to Dr. Tadesse, the camp's health programs at last were run almost entirely by their own people.

There was another reason REST wanted more of the camp people on the IRC payroll. The camp workers paid a portion of their salaries to REST as a sort of tax. This was done covertly; those IRC staff who were aware of the practice pretended not to know and accepted it as the price to pay for REST's cooperation. In fairness to REST, it should be stated that the money collected was spent on such things as blackboards and chalk for the makeshift schools established in camp, and clothing and sandals for the camp's more needy.

The IRC's relations with REST were for the most part cordial. Relations with the Sudanese COR, though also cordial in general, were quite often strained. Nevertheless, the COR officials on site at the camps proved to be friendly and often extremely helpful. The problems arose mostly out of disagreements with COR policy makers stationed in Gedaref town.

Ond of the bigger headaches between IRC and COR was policy regarding toilets. To dig an outdoor latrine, according to Sudanese Ministry of Health regulations, the hole must be dug "7 meters deep or until it hits water." The Fau camps were established by COR as "temporary" refugee reception centers as distinguished from "permanent" refugee settlements. According to COR, a latrine seven meters deep would be classified as a "permanent" structure, and the construction of permanent structures was disallowed at temporary reception centers.

Boy standing near water tanks, with Fau III in background.

Several alternative toilet designs were submitted, several compromises proposed, ideas to skirt the regulations considered. The IRC even promised to fill in all the latrines once the refugees went home. Each of the alternative designs was disallowed, all attempts at compromise foiled, ideas that sidestepped regulations dismissed. In the end, no latrines were built. The refugees used for a bathroom the open fields on the side of the camp opposite the canal. The area was quickly dubbed the "defecation fields." It was obvious that the defecation fields presented a health hazard and were the source of the terrific fly breeding.

The issue of the defecation fields and toilet building at Fau took many twists and turns down the negotiating path over the next several months, but was never resolved. Toilets continued to be an irritant in the relationship between IRC and COR.

Another policy disagreement arose between IRC and COR that eventually involved REST and UNHCR before it could be settled. At issue was whether to treat patients with tuberculosis.

A report by David Heiden at Fau III stated that

> Tuberculosis will soon be the leading cause of death (if not so
> already). . . . It is possible that even 5–10% of the camp may have
> active disease. . . . A decision to treat TB seems inevitable, and
> tentative planning should begin.

Dr. Rob Frey wrote in a report received in early April:

> [Tuberculosis] at Fau I . . . is now felt to be the number one killer
> of all patients, children and adults. . . .
>   [Plans to begin a TB treatment program have] been put on hold
> by COR/UNHCR until some procedural questions have been resolved.
> . . . We now have both the diagnostic laboratory capability and
> the medicines to begin. . . . We [should] organize a plan for
> management of this problem soon.

So why not treat patients who have tuberculosis? The argument
hinges on the nature of the organism that causes the disease and the
nature of its treatment. The disease is caused by *Mycobacterium
tuberculosis,* a bacterium that can be killed only very slowly. Because
of the relative ineffectiveness of the human immune response, a sustained chemical therapy is required. The usual treatment consists of
two weeks of daily injections followed by 12 months of daily pills of
Streptomycin and INH or rifampcin antibiotics.

Generally after the first two or three weeks of treatment, the patient displays remarkable improvement. A difficulty arises when the
patient begins to feel better — he may stop taking the daily medication before the course of treatment is complete. When this occurs, a
relapse is almost inevitable. The bacteria emerge stronger than ever,
often developing partial or even total resistance to the antibiotics,
thus rendering repeat treatment futile.

The demographic dynamics of famine are volatile to say the
least. The movement of refugees fleeing famine and crossing into
eastern Sudan even as late as April and May was tremendous.
Refugees from Tigre continued to cross the border at Wad Kowli and
at points farther north at rates in excess of 1,000 people per day. Also
many refugees already in the Sudan were talking about returning to
Tigre to prepare the fields for cultivation should the rains return. The
Fau camps were the most stable in eastern Sudan. Because of the

distance from the border, there were no new arrivals; the population was fixed. But even here REST had spread the word that it would direct a repatriation of refugees back to their homes in May to work in the fields.

With these movements in mind, COR was reluctant to allow treatment of TB to begin in the camps. If large numbers of refugees should default or discontinue their treatment because of demographic shifts, a more resistant, more deadly strain of TB bacteria could develop and might even spread to the Sudanese population.

The basic reasoning was sound, but in March and April, COR was more interested in asserting its authority over the foreign agencies than in reasoning with them. When Rob Frey and doctors from other organizations first approached COR about treatment for TB patients, Hassan Ossman, the head of COR for Sudan's Eastern Region, proclaimed that there was no tuberculosis in any of the refugee camps in eastern Sudan. This declaration provided a ready response for other COR authorities whenever the subject of treating tuberculosis was broached — why treat a disease that does not exist?

The word "tuberculosis" was banned from the vocabulary of reports. Even at meetings, COR officers would refuse to acknowledge verbal questions mentioning "tuberculosis." Doctors were made to know that if they wanted to talk about tuberculosis, they would have to use the term "chronic disease."

Even Western doctors were not of one mind concerning the treatment of TB in a refugee setting. The IRC's Dr. Peter Krewet at Fau I had worked with Ethiopian refugees in Somalia and had witnessed an unacceptably high default rate among the refugees there. Dr. Richard Nesbitt, the head of UNHCR's medical unit, understood both sides of the argument and agonized over the decision.

While TB policies were being debated at the administrative level, the relief workers in the camps saw young men wasting away, old women coughing up blood, and little children growing weak and dying. For these workers, the long-term consequences of a possible resistant strain developing from defaulters were irrelevant. People were dying, and the medicines that would cure them were sitting only a few yards away in unopened boxes in the pharmacy. The issue became emotionally charged.

Finally, after several rounds of negotiations, REST promised that, even if the other refugees returned home, anyone diagnosed with tuberculosis and begun on treatment would remain in the Sudan until the full 12-month course of treatment was completed. Following this assurance, the welcome announcement was made by Dr. Nabil of COR. TB treatment was begun, and the death rate in the camps further declined.

In the first few months of 1985, the Sudanese economy had fallen into total collapse. A $9 billion foreign debt, a 25 percent annual inflation rate, vanishing revenues, and the cruelty of a multi-year drought had led to import restrictions, a freeze on foreign currency accounts, rationing of fuel, and even rationing and restrictions on the sale of basic food commodities. The Sudan had recently acknowledged its own famine and was soliciting international assistance for famine relief in both the Eastern Region bordering Ethiopia and the Western Region bordering Chad. Thousands of displaced persons had fled the famine-affected desert Western Region and were camped on the outskirts of Khartoum. Journalists equated the situation in the Sudan with that of Ethiopia.

The Sudan's Southern Region suffered under the resurgence of civil war. The conflict had been simmering for 12 years, but erupted again with the 1983 establishment of Islamic or Sharia Law, which the mostly Christian South regarded as an infringement on its autonomy. The Southern rebels attacked Chevron's main oil drilling site. Chevron subsequently suspended its billion-dollar operations, further contributing to the economic collapse.

The Sudan's president, Jafaar Nmeiri, had managed to hold onto the reins of power for 16 years without the legitimacy of elections. Nmeiri's authority had never been absolute; he held his position through manipulation and by compromising with the factions most threatening at the moment. Most recently, he had been capitulating to the Muslim Brotherhood, a group tied to international fundamentalist Islamic movements, by introducing the Sharia in September 1983, and submitting several proposals, all rejected by the Sudanese Assembly, to further the creation of a full Islamic Republic. Ann Mosely Lesch noted in *Foreign Affairs* that

> ...Businessmen were also alienated by the regime's corrupt practises, and military officers resented Nmeiri's frequent, politically

motivated purges of the officer corps. By April 1985, Nmeiri had offended nearly all the political and military forces in Sudan. [*A View from Khartoum,* reprinted by permission of *Foreign Affairs* (Spring, 1987). Copyright 1987 by the Council on Foreign Relations, Inc.]

In the spring of 1985, Nmeiri's hold on power seemed more tenuous than ever. The middle classes had grown disenchanted with government by dictatorship and yearned for democracy.

Then, during the first week of April, President Nmeiri was overthrown in a coup d'état. Only two weeks earlier, a "high ranking United States diplomat," the usual journalistic pseudonym for ambassador, had described Nmeiri to *Newsweek* reporters as the "Master of Khartoum."

For five days in a row, the relief workers at Fau, sitting on wooden planks and empty OXFAM Energy Biscuit containers, clustered around the shortwave radio at seven o'clock A.M. and six o'clock P.M. for the BBC's World News broadcasts. The first day mentioned massive demonstrations and riots in the streets of Khartoum and the closure of the Khartoum airport. There were rumors that the overthrow of Nmeiri was imminent. Nmeiri himself was out of the country on a visit to the United States.

For the next three days, the BBC opened its international reports with the words, "Khartoum remains virtually shut off from the outside world." Roads were closed, telex and telephone communications were down, even the post office was closed.

The relief workers were worried. If the Nmeiri dictatorship were overthrown, what sort of government would replace him? The Communists were active in the Sudan, but they were not strong. The Muslim Brotherhood had a strong base of support and would grab power if they could. For Westerners in the Sudan, this would be the worst turn of events. Palestinians, Libyans, and extremist Arab groups were already highly visible in Khartoum. Should the Muslim Brothers seize power in Khartoum and the United States refuse to extradite Nmeiri, anti–Western sentiments would be unleashed.

Concern and uneasiness showed on the faces of the relief workers, but their fears remained largely unspoken. They remembered that the emergency evacuation plan called for them to take a vehicle up to the northeast to Port Sudan on the Red Sea — a 14-hour drive from Fau.

More than about their own personal safety, the relief workers were worried about what would happen to the refugees. Whoever seized political power in the Sudan might blame them for the collapse of the economy. Latent resentments might erupt into open hostilities. A society disintegrating under economic and political failure could easily turn violent, and the most convenient targets would be the refugees.

On the fifth day, the BBC announced that Nmeiri had flown to Cairo. Later it reported that General Abd al-Rahman Siwar al-Dhahab, Nmeiri's newly appointed Minister of Defense, had seized power.

It had been a revolution in that the demonstrations had brought everyone into the streets — merchants as well as students, professional people as well as radicals. The middle class had joined in the call for change.

No revolutionary changes would result from this transfer of power, however. Only the head of state had been overthrown, not the entire government. The military had taken over the administration of government, and the military was conservative.

Siwar al-Dhahab called for changes in internal government functionings and bureaucracies. But he was a moderate; he called for a sharing of power with civilians, the composition of a constitution, and democratic elections to be held within 12 months. He reformed the currency and put limits on wage increases in the public sector. His actions reassured his countrymen and foreign observers as well. Policy affecting refugees remained unchanged.

Since October of 1984, REST had insisted that the refugees entering the Sudan would stay for only a few months before returning home. Every few weeks, rumors circulated among the refugees in the camps of an impending repatriation, but none of the relief workers expected the refugees to go home anytime soon. The flood of newly arriving refugees from Tigre continued to pour into the Sudan well into 1985. *Refugees* magazine stated that "in addition to the 87,000 individuals who had arrived in 1984, there were 60,500 new arrivals in January, 36,000 in February, 45,000 in March, 33,000 in April. . ." (Annick Billard, "Eastern Sudan: Huge Efforts Paying Off,"

Refugees no. 27 [March 1986], p. 20). The incoming flow of refugees would have to stop before anyone could think of returning home.

Because of the disaster that had occurred at Tuklebab and the frequency of encounters with government warplanes on the Tuklebab road, in late December REST began to lead the incoming refugees along a different, more southerly route into the Sudan that terminated near a tiny Sudanese village called Wad Kowli. By March, more than 92,000 Tigreans had descended upon Wad Kowli. The Atbara River, the only water source, was quickly exhausted. Three 45,000-litre tankers trucked water into the camp from a deep pool in the river bed some 28 miles away, but this system was devised when the camp population was 20,000 people. It was barely sufficient then; it was woefully inadequate now.

Because of the lack of water, evacuation of the camp began in late March, but the new arrivals entering Wad Kowli, 1,000 to 3,000 people per day, outnumbered those transferred to other sites. Eventually, about 35,000 refugees were moved from Wad Kowli to other sites, but even after the transfers the population of Wad Kowli neared 100,000.

With the overthrow of Nmeiri, Jerry Weaver, the United States embassy's Refugee Affairs Coordinator, departed from the Sudan in a hurry — he would be in danger once the details of his CIA-run airlift of Ethiopian Jews were discovered by Sudan's new leaders. He was replaced by Frank Moss, who was eager to demonstrate United States concern for the famine refugees. One of his first achievements was to organize nine more tanker trucks to haul water to Wad Kowli.

This United States assistance helped prevent a major disaster at Wad Kowli, but the situation there was still bleak. Death rates at Wad Kowli approached those recorded during the terrible winter months at Fau. And still the flood of new arrivals into Wad Kowli continued.

Then, in the first week of May, the influx of refugees into Wad Kowli stopped almost overnight. Meanwhile, at Fau, REST began registering people to return to Tigre. They had called for volunteers to return to plow and sow the land in preparation for the rainy season. The response was great; many of the refugees who signed up were delighted at the chance to leave behind these horrid, dusty camps in the Sudan and go home.

The idea of repatriation of refugees back to Tigre in May was at first greeted with disbelief by the relief workers. These people, though in better health than they were five months ago, seemed in no condition to walk for weeks to return to empty villages without food.

Though REST representatives insisted that the registrants were all volunteers, at least some of the people who signed up did so as a result of coercion put forth by REST upon their families. Two teenage girls at Fau II told me, through interpreters, that REST had ordered the people to send at least one able-bodied person from each household to prepare the land for cultivation. These girls would be leaving their families behind at Fau II and journeying back to Tigre only because of REST's intimidation.

The IRC teams set up repatriation medical screening centers at each Fau camp to determine who was and who wasn't medically fit to go. This more or less consisted of finding out whether the registrant was a TB patient who had begun treatment.

Throughout the whole process, REST members in camp couldn't say when the move would begin; nor could they say where they would be getting the necessary trucks and fuel. All along the relief workers asked each other, "Do you think any of them will really go?"

Then one morning in mid–May at Fau III, I was awakened by one of our nurses who had gone into camp shortly after dawn. "The trucks are here," she said. "The refugees are starting to leave."

We entered the camp and watched the trucks being loaded with their human cargo from a distance. We weren't involved in this operation, and we continued to have misgivings about the fate of the people so happily boarding the lorries.

For several weeks following, at Fau III, then at Fau II, then at Fau I, 19 Bedford lorries shuttled back and forth between Fau and Wad Kowli, the point of disembarkation. Repatriation also occurred from Wad Kowli and from the other newly established camps such as Safawa and Hilat Hakuma. By the middle of June, approximately 55,000 Tigreans who had come to the Sudan since the emergency had returned to Tigre to prepare the fields and sow crops. About 13,600 of these had left from Fau.

As we watched them board the lorries day after day, we couldn't help our pessimism. The rains had failed for so many years; why should anyone believe they would return this year? What would happen to these people who seemed so excited and eager to go home? What would they find? Deserted villages, looted homes, barren land, renewed suffering and despair? How many would die before they reached their destination? If the rains failed again, what would happen to them? If the rains failed again... It was too awful to think of.

Meanwhile, our work continued. Some 6,700 people still remained at Fau III, 7,800 at Fau II, and 6,800 at Fau I. The tents abandoned by the returnees were filled by others and a general consolidation at each camp was achieved. The tents were made less crowded, and at Fau III the tiny straw hovels that had constituted section G were removed altogether.

Local COR officials had sufficient latitude to make decisions regarding the appearance of the camps. Our sanitation teams had tried at each Fau camp to begin a tree-planting and home gardening project. The COR administrators at Fau II and Fau III disallowed the projects because they considered trees to be permanent structures, but the COR officers at Fau I embraced the idea. In June, 1,000 trees supplied by CARE were planted, one at each tent, and were now growing and cared for by the refugees. The green color and the idea of any vegetation growing at all provided the camp a much more livable atmosphere. The outpatient and inpatient clinic, TB and feeding center, laboratory and pharmacy had all been rebuilt under the direction of Craig Stein in a layout complete with flower gardens.

In late May, I moved back to Fau I after an absence of nearly two months to train a new lab technician, the former one having quit his job because of ethnic harassment. It was after I entered the inpatient ward that I witnessed the most amazing change. A boy of 13 or 14 years, a strong, muscular youth, ran up and put his arms around me. It was all very odd until I looked down into the boy's face. Could it be Nagassy? He had put on at least 30 pounds, had actually grown several inches, and even appeared several years older. He was the picture of health — not the skin-stretched skeleton of before. But it certainly was Nagassy. No one could fail to recognize the gentle smile, the warm eyes.

Coached by sanitarian Dick Bauer and Dr. Neil Biust, Nagassy had gained a vocabulary of about 25 English words. Imagine my surprise when he looked up and said in English, "Hello. How are you. I'm fine."

Perhaps because of the language barrier, there had always seemed a certain distance between the relief workers and the camp refugees. The Western relief workers developed their closest relationships with the workers whom they trained, mostly Amharas from outside the camp. Making friends inside the camp was more difficult. I once randomly stopped in at a tent at Fau II on my way from the clinic to the expatriate living compound. After about 15 minutes of smiles, sign language, and the dozen or so words of Tigrenia I'd picked up, I left. My hosts were gracious enough, but the expression in their faces at my departure seemed to say, "Why did you come here?"

Eventually, most of us did develop friendships in camp, often by playing with the children and then meeting their parents. Language continued to be a barrier, especially as none of the relief workers spoke more than cursory Tigrenia. Few adult refugees knew any English at all. Some of the children, however, commanded a surprising degree of language ability. Ben Curran, camp manager at Fau II, received the following letter from one of the refugee children. Treasures like this made all the hardships and sacrifice worthwhile.

Dear Sir

Mr. Ben:

I am an Ethiopian refugee especially from Tigre Province where I lived here meanwhile in Fau II Reception Center and also almost for 1 year, but you lived with us for 6 months you did so many things as far as you can, you helped the refugees from hunger and death. The people of Tigre willn't forget you in his mind for the future.
But I would miss you!!
I wish you a nice future in usa. One day we will be together. I am 12 years old.

Yours sincerely,

Tekelay Girma

Nagassy at Fau I was a treasure for us all. He understood the meaning of what was said even if he didn't understand the words. He worked in the inpatient wards now as a paid local employee (making about $25 a month), doing odd jobs and making himself as useful as possible. He was often employed as an interpreter, to explain things to patients and put them at ease — he had been through it all himself.

Nagassy seemed to symbolize all that had occurred at Fau in the past six months. He had lost his family, but he had found new friends in the relief workers. He had been given no hope, but now he was cared for. He had been left to die, but now if you asked him, he would reply in English, "I'm fine."

In April, May, and June, the convection of the tremendous desert heat and the ever-present wind combined to form tiny but powerful whirlwinds or "dust-devils" like miniature tornadoes. You could see the swirling dust form columns high in the sky from miles away. Occasionally they would blow into camp and follow an erratic path through the tents. They were always cause for excitement since, more often than not, they would uproot a couple of tents and send them billowing into the sky — a not too subtle reminder of how fragile was the refugees' existence here, how utterly their lives were dependent on forces beyond their control.

On May 28 at about five o'clock in the afternoon, the wind picked up even more strongly than usual. Within 10 minutes a high velocity blast was blowing up thick clouds of dust and debris, blocking the sun from view. The temperature dropped at least 20 degrees, and the wind continued to blow dusty grit through the air and to howl interminably.

It was a dust storm such as I'd never experienced. Dr. Peter Krewet and I were the only ones at the Fau I compound at the time. Nothing could be heard in the wind; we had to shout at the top of our lungs to make ourselves understood. The gusts continued to blast away and only increased in intensity.

For 45 minutes the dust and wind storm blew, and then suddenly big drops of rain splattered down from the sky. Even while the wind continued unabated, the rain burst into torrents, swirling wildly and pounding relentlessly.

"Rain! Rain!" I thought. Could this be the end of the drought? I wondered if the refugees were laughing and dancing in the rain.

The nurses arrived from camp drenched and covered with mud on the back of the Toyota pickup. They were in a terrific state of excitement. "It's dreadful!" they cried. "All the tents have blown down. Some of the refugees are trying to put them back up, but it's useless.

Some of them blew all the way across the canal and are gone. There's nothing to be done. They'll have to sleep in the rain and the mud. There's nothing we can do to help."

It rained till well past midnight. It rained again about a week later and again a few days after that. Fortunately, the violence of the first storm never repeated itself.

Rumors abounded that it was raining in Tigre as well. The repatriation and the effort to plow and sow the fields might prove to be successful endeavors after all. We all awaited what the next few months would bring.

IX. July–December 1985

In the first week of June 1985, I discovered I had hepatitis.

After a painfully bumpy ride in the Landcruiser, I made it into Khartoum and was promptly checked into the Khartoum Clinic, where I remained for three weeks. The Khartoum Clinic in June was a waystation for nearly all the relief workers in the Sudan: three cases of typhoid, two of amebiasis, one giardia, one malaria, one schistosomiasis, and several fevers of unknown origin all made their way to the clinic during my stay. Several of these were IRC workers from Fau. As the afternoon temperatures in late May and June reached intolerable highs of up to 135°F, the relief workers drank more and more water, which was not always sanitary. The increased water consumption led directly to higher incidences of illness.

In my weakened condition I was no good to anyone, so it was decided that I would be sent home, to return to the Sudan in five or six weeks or whenever my blood tests returned to normal.

Back in the United States, interest in the Great Famine had reached its peak. "We Are the World" albums were selling briskly, and the "Live-Aid" rock concert was held on July 13. Every newspaper and magazine contained accounts of the famine. I was impressed with the level of awareness and concern.

Most of the people with whom I talked were extremely interested and curious to hear what was happening in eastern Sudan. My friends and relatives and their acquaintances bombarded me with questions. The KMOX radio in St. Louis interviewed me over the telephone. In answering their questions, I found it very hard to convey the difficulties encountered in the aid and relief operations.

First, imagine a place where there is no electricity — no electric lights at night, no air conditioning or even electric fans in temperatures as high as 135°F, no refrigerators, no electric or gas stoves so that all meals are cooked on charcoal or wood fires, and no telephones to communicate with anyone further than walking distance away. Imagine a postal system where letters can take several weeks and often are not delivered at all. Imagine transportation in a place with no roads, few automobiles, and rationed fuel. Imagine a place with no industry or business at all, no jobs, no amusements, no doctors or hospitals, no food, no money, nothing. Now, imagine all the problems that would stem, directly and indirectly, from such conditions. No wonder Americans had difficulty appreciating the difficulties encountered in the aid and relief operations in eastern Sudan: They first had to imagine a context that was completely alien.

Maintenance of vehicles was a problem of top priority. Because of the lack of an adequate postal system and no working telephones, we not only moved people and supplies with our vehicles, but we depended on our vehicles as our only system of communications. Without the vehicles, communications would break down completely — as would the entire relief effort.

Because there were no roads other than the paved road linking Fau II to Khartoum and to Gedaref town, our vehicles rapidly deteriorated under the bumps, jolts, and cruelty of cross-country driving. Tires suffered the most, rolling constantly over acacia thorns that littered the hard ground. The heat dessicated the lubrication system and the dust worked its way into every joint, sucking up oil like a sponge. In the course of a few weeks, our vehicles endured the wear and tear of several years of hard driving.

Because there were few automobiles in the Sudan, auto-parts stores were non-existent. Parts were imported at exorbitant costs. Months might pass between the time of ordering and the time of delivery. Vehicles stood idle for lack of simple parts. Many usable vehicles were cannibalized to free up parts for other vehicles. The UNHCR set up a vehicle repair shop near Gedaref town, but it suffered the same problems the relief organizations faced: high costs and long delivery times.

Also because there were so few automobiles in the Sudan, there were very few automobile mechanics. Finding one or several mechanics who could work reasonably well with automobiles was a challenge to all the relief organizations in the Sudan.

Oil, diesel, and benzine were all in such short supply that they were subject to government rationing. Without oil and fuel, there was no point in attempting vehicle maintenance. Relief organizations were forced to restrict vehicle usage to a minimum in times of shortages, and the effect was felt in program operations.

Vehicle maintenance was only one of several problems difficult to explain to someone unfamiliar with the context of the circumstances in eastern Sudan. Other examples could be cited. Imagine, for instance, the political implications of importing expensive tuberculosis medicines to be given to Ethiopian refugees in eastern Sudan when the local Sudanese population did not have access to these medications or, indeed, to even a minimal health care delivery system.

The press helped to damage the image of relief workers and relief organizations by highlighting alleged misappropriation of funds in January by International Christian Aid, a part of Inter-Aid, Inc., based in Camarillo, California. Inter-Aid had indeed contributed food, medicines, and a vehicle to the international relief effort at the time of the blowup in the media. The confusion had resulted from Inter-Aid's not being registered with the Ethiopian government as a relief agency. The organization, instead, had chosen to funnel its aid through an umbrella group, Christian Relief and Developent Association, which was already registered with the Ethiopian government. Inter-Aid had, in fact, provided funds and supplies for famine relief, but the correction did not make the headlines as the original accusations did.

While I was in the United States in the summer of 1985, some of my friends asked me about other newspaper reports of grain sitting idly on board ships or in warehouses. They didn't realize that, while donor countries were happy to send over excess grain (which was often less expensive than storing it), they often fell short of providing sufficient funding to purchase fuel and vehicles and parts for transport. The flood of food aid into countries with limited infrastructure simply exceeded the capacity of the distribution system. And while it was easy to solicit donors for grain, it was another matter to solicit funding for salaries of the necessary personnel: loaders, inventory clerks, drivers, mechanics, logistics coordinators, accountants, etc.

Some of my friends asked about reports of medicines spoiling while in storage. They didn't realize that, while relief agencies could easily find donors to contribute money to buy medicines, they found it difficult to obtain funds to construct refrigerated storerooms and the electric generators required to keep them in operation. Nor could they find donors willing to purchase plane tickets for relief workers or pay the salaries of local workers being trained to dispense supplies. Some supplies did spoil — surprisingly few, however, considering that the only storage areas consisted of canvas tents and grass huts with little ability to keep out the rats, or the heat, or the rain.

I was familiar with a $30,000 donation made by a church group which stipulated that the monies be spent exclusively on medical and sanitation supplies. The terms of the donation explicitly stated that the funds were not to be used for rental properties or for local workers' salaries. Many donors, afraid of waste or mismanagement, put similar restrictions on the use of donated funds. At the time this particular donation was made, our storerooms were overflowing with medical and sanitation supplies, but we were having problems negotiating the rent on the Gedaref field office, and we were laying off local workers as funds for local salaries were running thin.

Some people felt that the local workers who benefited from services provided ought to volunteer their work without pay. As policy such idealism would be impossible to implement. We could never have enticed the English-speaking refugees from Gedaref town to come to work at Fau without some sort of remuneration. And, as for the camp refugees, the salaries were small, $30–35 a month on average. Besides, wasn't this the most direct form of aid possible — putting money directly in the pockets of the refugees? And it was fascinating to see the circulation of the money in camp. A tiny economy started to develop. People at Fau I, who had been wearing rags sewn together from empty grain sacks, suddenly began appearing in new clothes purchased from nearby Sudanese Tenedba village. Little coffee and tea shops sprang up around the perimeter of camp. Soon tailor shops followed, and tiny shops offering ball-point pens and bubble gum. Some women took in laundry and with the money they earned purchased goat meat for their families from Sudanese Village Three about five miles across the canal from Fau II. Schools for the children were established and an orphanage set up by REST from the tax received out of local workers' salaries.

Some of my friends were appalled when I mentioned that at each

Fau compound IRC employed a cook and a maid to do the laundry. They didn't realize how absurd it would be for the relief workers to spend the better part of the day cooking meals over a charcoal fire and washing clothes by hand in a bucket over a concrete slab. The $25/month salary of a laundress for the compound was well worth the time it freed for the relief workers to remain in camp. Nor could it be said that living in a straw hut in the Sudanese desert at Fau or in a concrete apartment in the slum of Gedaref town, even with a cook or a maid, was ever luxurious.

I was not aware of any Western relief workers who grew rich from their salaries. Some organizations paid more than others. The UNHCR was known to pay its Western staff above-average salaries. Directors of some agencies lived in comfortable quarters in Khartoum, but all of these top administrative officers could have been earning far more at home. I was well acquainted with one relief worker who, against the advice of all his family and friends, turned down a job offer as chief financial officer of a hospital in Louisiana in order to come to work in the Sudan for less than half the pay.

I remained at my home in Belleville, Illinois, for six weeks in June and July, recovering from hepatitis. It rained often during this time, and after six months of Sudanese dust, I was amazed at how green everything was at home. The corn and beans in the farmers' fields sparkled in neat green rows, and the hardwood trees in the forests shimmered in the heat and humidity of emerald afternoons — a typically verdant Midwest summer.

The temptation to draw comparisons was unavoidable. How different were the lives led at the same point in time by human beings through accident of birth and chance of geography! The contrast between the freshly cut lawns in Illinois and the hard, cracked earth between the tents at Fau was as stark as that between the applauding spectators at the Live-Aid Concert munching nachos, Pepsi, and hot dogs and the long lines of refugees patiently waiting for their ten-day allotment of dried beans, lentils, and flour in front of the COR distribution tent.

To most people, perhaps, the dusty refugee camps seemed distant — somewhere off in Africa, far, far away. I was keenly aware that with a few hours on a plane followed by a few hours in a Landcruiser, the pitiful images on the television screen could suddenly cease to be pictures — they were real people, in misery, and not really so far away.

On July 25, I boarded a Pan-Am carrier to take me those few hours to Khartoum. The city was dry and dusty as usual. At the IRC office I was told that it had been raining in the Eastern Region, three or four days per week since the end of June.

The road to Fau followed a course along the Blue Nile for the first three hours. The river was about three times wider than it had been two months earlier and now was near to overflowing its banks.

Just outside of El Fau town, the dusty countryside underwent a radical transformation. Where two months ago there had stretched endless horizons of dust, there now were planted fields of wheat, sorghum, and sesame growing bright green with water glistening in the furrows. Land that had stood as empty desert not long ago now grew full of tall grasses, green and tossing in the breeze.

Between the town of El Fau and Fau III refugee camp the road traversed a rocky, sandy stretch, and here the grass was shorter but no less green. In one area a type of wild flower covered the ground with blossoms so white and so numerous that, from a distance, they looked like snow. The leafless thornbushes that I had always assumed were dead now displayed pea-green leaves and tiny yellow blossoms. Dragonflies of blazing jet blue and green could be seen by the hundreds buzzing over the tops of the two-foot-tall reeds and grasses.

Birds soared everywhere. Crows, blackbirds, and hawks sailed through the air and lined the roadsides. Flocks of white egrets fluttered aimlessly. Maribou storks strutted defiantly in sandy clearings. Majestic white ibises spread their wings and took to the air in effortless flight. Halfway to Fau III an eagle took flight from its perch in the top of a tall, dead tree. The bird was so large that it made the treelimbs creak under the strain and gave the illusion that the whole top half of the tree had just flown away.

In the camps, the tents were half hidden by grass and the walkways muddy and slippery with puddles. The refugees had adjusted to the change in the seasons. They built up the floors in their tents to keep the rain from draining in. Many of them constructed small, two-foot-high earthen walls in front of their tents to protect their cooking fires from the wind-driven rain.

The relief workers had draped plastic sheets over the straw roof of the clinic and over other IRC buildings in an attempt to keep out the rain. The clinics were still crowded: The rain had brought more mosquitoes and the mosquitoes had brought more malaria. In general, though, the health of the refugees continued to improve. The UNHCR had declared an end to the emergency in eastern Sudan, although it recognized that 300,000 Ethiopian refugees remained in the Sudan still completely dependent on outside assistance for survival.

The rains came every two, three or four days and usually occurred in the evening or during the night. On the days after a particularly heavy rain, work came to a virtual standstill. Vehicles were useless and transportation between camps impossible. The relief workers walked into camp barefoot to prevent losing a sandal in the deep mud. The clay soil caked together when wet and stuck in heavy globs to their feet so that walking even a short distance was a chore.

The rains did bring cooler weather. The temperature in August seldom exceeded 100°F. This was a welcome relief from the suffocating temperatures of May and June.

The greatest gift of the rainy season was the total disappearance of the flies. The maddening pests were gone. Nobody knew why, though there was some discussion of maggots drowning in standing water and birds devouring large numbers of adults. In any case, the flies had vanished, and that in itself improved conditions in the camps one thousand fold for relief workers and refugees alike.

The IRC programs had been fully staffed since the end of May, and the severe shortage of sanitation and managerial personnel had been remedied. As a result, substantial improvements in living conditions for both refugees and relief workers had been made.

Drinking water, though muddier than ever because of the rains, was finally chlorinated sufficiently on an everyday basis. Insecticides were used effectively and judiciously. Sanitation program cleaning crews of camp refugees roamed through the camps cutting and burning weeds and collecting and burying garbage.

In the relief workers' living quarters compound, new grass huts were constructed, the inside walls were whitewashed, a barrel shower was installed at each compound, common areas were enlarged, brick or crushed rock floors were laid down, small generators were purchased to provide electric lighting in the common dining

Girl at Fau III preparing a meal of lentils.

rooms, and at Fau III the ultimate luxury was indulged in with the construction of a vented corrugated tin outhouse.

A manager was in charge of each camp now to coordinate the various programs and the use of vehicles, to purchase food and other provisions, to negotiate with COR and REST on day-to-day policy issues, to keep records, and to coordinate communications with the Gedaref field office regarding supplies, logistics, and other program needs. Such personnel had been sorely missed earlier.

It was evident that the programs ran more smoothly now, and the evidence showed up in the mortality rates. The death rates for the rainy season months were as follows: July, 27 deaths/10,000 population; August, 20/10,000; and September, 10.7/10,000.

On a more subjective basis, the refugees just seemed healthier. At Fau I a tiny handicrafts industry had evolved — refugees produced decorated straw baskets and embroideries and became actively involved in marketing their wares. The REST and camp refugees were negotiating with Sudanese landowners to work in the fields at harvest time. A vibrancy issued from the camps now quite unlike the despondency of earlier days.

The coming of the rains itself produced positive psychological effects on the refugees' health, but the major reasons for the improvement in health at the camps were the now continuous and reliable supplies of food and medicines and the safe potable water supply. In addition, the increase in the number of Western professional health workers and the decrease in the refugee population through the May repatriations allowed a more favorable health worker to refugee ratio. The cumulative effect on the health programs, medical, sanitation, nutrition, and public health, was that the teams who managed them were able to plan and set objectives rather than to react to one crisis after another in a haphazard fashion.

A noticeable improvement in the refugees' personal hygiene had been effected. Refugees constantly asked public health workers for an increase in soap distribution for washing.

Often all that a program needed was a little innovation. Scott Dethloff noticed that few of the refugees at Fau III washed their clothes. It had always been assumed that the reason for this was that the refugees didn't have a change of clothes — they couldn't wash what they needed to wear. After a little investigation, Scott discovered that the real reason was that there was no place to dry the clothes after washing. There were no trees and few thornbushes. Refugees who did wash their clothes spread them out on the ground to dry and in the process picked up so much mud that the clothes ended up dirtier than they were to begin with. Scott drove out to El Fau town, bought $50 worth of rope, and strung clotheslines between all the tents at Fau III. Suddenly everyone was washing clothes.

In June and July, the sanitation, medical, and public health teams coordinated efforts for a program to prevent and contain the disease that was expected with dread as the rainy season progressed: cholera.

Reports had reached IRC workers as early as May of cholera epidemics killing hundreds of Ethiopian refugees in camps in Somalia and at feeding centers in Tigre itself. Of all potential health concerns, cholera was the most feared in this type of setting. No other infectious disease could kill so many people in so short a period.

The IRC sanitarian Anna Helms had submitted specific proposals in May for the prevention of the disease at Fau. Her recommendations were used as the basis of the cholera prevention and containment measures put into effect in July.

In Gedaref town, the purchasing staff scoured the market for lime for use in disinfection. In the camps, sanitarians erected separate shelters containing beds to house and isolate cholera patients. They also excavated flyproof waste-disposal pits, and they delivered instructions in disinfection techniques using soap and bleaching powder solutions to refugee workers who would come in contact with the patients and who would handle kitchen utensils. Public health workers began a community-wide public health education effort; the people in the camps learned to recognize symptoms and to summon a public health home visitor whenever a family member showed signs of the disease.

Other organizations working in other refugee camps in the Eastern Region took similar precautions. At the monthly interagency meeting held outside of Gedaref town, cholera and its prevention were the sole topics of interest. Everyone realized the danger; once an epidemic started, it would be difficult to contain, and loss of life would be tremendous. These meagre refugee camps wallowing in the mud were easy targets—cholera epidemics just waiting to happen.

Officials of COR were as concerned as anyone else, though for different reasons. Cholera would occur in Sudan's villages as it had every year from time immemorial, but if epidemics occurred in the refugee camps, there would be a strong feeling that the refugees had brought the disease with them and COR would be blamed for failing to contain the disease.

The COR "solved" the problem the same way it had solved the tuberculosis problem a few months earlier. All the agencies were told that cholera did not exist in the camps, nor would it exist in the camps anytime in the future. At no time was the word "cholera" to be used in reports or even in conversation. Suspected cases were to be referred to as "001"—a term derived from the 01 serogroup of the cholera bacteria most common in the Sudan.

In the end, all the planning and prevention efforts paid off handsomely. The dreaded cholera epidemics never materialized. It was an instructive realization of what proper planning and adequate preparation can achieve.

The disease was present in the camps. At Fau, from July through September, nearly two dozen suspected cases were treated; several of these were confirmed. Only a few deaths were attributed to cholera, but none of these could be confirmed. The story was the same in the other refugee camps in eastern Sudan: The cholera epidemics had been averted.

A small Sudanese village known only as "Village 36" was not so lucky. There cholera had struck in force. The village lay just a short distance from the tarmac road between Fau II and Fau III. The Sudanese government had posted one health worker in the village, and he was quickly overwhelmed. A message for help from Village 36 reached IRC's Dr. Rich Kovar at Fau III. Over the next several weeks, the IRC staff stationed at Fau III spent most of their time working at Village 36.

Although it was widely known among relief workers that the health status of Sudanese villages was poor and that the health services provided to them were inadequate, the conditions at Village 36 were shocking to the IRC workers who commuted there from Fau III. Little food was to be found, and absolutely no medicines. Sanitation was completely lacking. There were no latrines in the village, and there was no system to purify the drinking water. Often children scooped drinking water from the large pools of muddy rainwater along the footpaths. Another child might have defecated in the same water only minutes earlier. No wonder cholera thrived here.

"The people of Village 36 are worse off than the people at Fau III," lamented Rulester Davis, an IRC nutritionist who tried in August to help the most malnourished children of Village 36 by using extra food supplies from Fau III.

By late September, the cholera outbreak at Village 36 had abated, and the IRC workers returned to Fau III full-time.

The relief agencies providing assistance to refugees in the Sudan have often been unfairly criticized for ignoring the plight of the local Sudanese. Such criticism is usually voiced by Sudanese government officials. In fact, though many agencies are commissioned through the Sudanese government only to provide services to refugees, substantial help does make its way to the local populace. The work accomplished at Village 36 is an example of refugee relief agency personnel providing assistance wherever it is needed.

Work continued at all the Fau camps throughout the rainy season. The rains, which usually lasted several hours, fell every three or four days. At Fau II and Fau III, transportation was only slightly impeded since the tarmac road lay so near to the camps. At Fau I, however, the nearest paved road ran 20 miles from the camp.

Transportation to and from Fau I grew progressively more difficult as the rainy season wore on.

A muddy dirt road connected Fau I to Fau II; a back road wound through the mud and scattered acacia forests from Fau I all the way to Gedaref town. The only traffic on these two roads was the IRC Landcruisers and the big Bedford supply lorries. The lorries plowed through the mud, sometimes sinking up to their wheel axles. The heavy lorries left huge, deep ruts in the soft earth that filled with water after a rain and rendered driving treacherous for the IRC vehicles. Even without the ruts, driving after a rain was impossible on these mud roads—the oozing, clay soil swallowed up spinning tires.

In late August, it rained for four days straight, and the roads to Fau I became totally impassable. For seven full days, communications with the camp were completely shut off. The workers at Fau II and Fau III grew increasingly uneasy about their counterparts. If there was an emergency, a snakebite. . . .

On the eighth day, in the afternoon, some of the local staff rushed into the clinic at Fau II, laughing and carrying the news that Fau I was coming on camels. Dr. Steve Bickler had organized a camel caravan to get out of Fau I and into El Fau town to buy provisions. What a sight to see the entire foreign staff from Fau I plodding through the mud on a long line of camels like so many Sudanese nomads!

By late September, the rains were diminishing. The surrounding fields of sorghum and sesame were green and growing tall. Grass and weeds grew in between the tents, partially hiding them from view. Refugee sanitation workers cut the weeds down with scythes. Anyone who had seen the dust and desolation of a few months ago would have found the transformation amazing.

The relief operations were running more smoothly now, and the refugees seemed healthier and happier. Water was chlorinated and stored in clean metal tanks at several distribution sites. There were still no latrines, but at least there was a defined area designated for defecation which the refugee sanitation workers cleaned once per week. Food was not plentiful, nor was it appetizing, but nobody went hungry. There were plenty of medicines and trained health workers around for those who were sick. The public health program employed home visitors who visited each tent in camp every single day — through them, the community had been made aware of public health hazards and educated in disease prevention and personal hygiene.

The flies had vanished, but wasps, hornets, "blister beetles," praying mantises, and swarms of crickets and other insect pests kept outdoor life interesting. Because of the standing water, mosquitoes bred and the incidence of malaria increased.

Several days were spent in early October using the laboratory at Fau II to conduct a malaria survey. The findings confirmed that approximately 40 percent of high-grade fevers in camp were caused by malaria. As a result of the survey, the medical and public health teams began preventative treatment of chloroquine prophylaxis. By now, the camps were stocked with ample supplies of chloroquine and all the other necessary medicines.

By September, conditions had improved so much that the programs began to be scaled back. When Western relief workers left at the expiration of their contracts, they were not replaced, and thus the expatriate presence was allowed to diminish through attrition.

The local staff was reduced by half in late September. The reduction was made almost entirely among the Amharic workers, which helped lessen the ethnic tensions in camp. Program supervisors were reluctant to send so many of their workers away to Gedaref town or Khartoum where prospects for employment were bleak, but even the workers themselves conceded that their services were no longer called for. The health needs in camp, though still apparent, were nowhere near the crisis levels of only a few months before.

Cutting back the programs was much easier than building them up. Because of the smaller number of refugees in camp after May's repatriation and the improving health status of those remaining, the scaling down of programs went unnoticed or was accepted as a necessary adaptation. Having grown accustomed to the services, however, a few refugees were reluctant to give them up.

In April and May, patients with tuberculosis were actively sought out and removed to the TB center, where they would remain for several weeks until they were rendered non-infectious through medication and where they could regain their lost weight through extra feeding rations. This practice continued throughout the rainy season. By October, few new TB cases were being discovered, TB patients already at the center were gaining strength, and the medical team decided to try to speed up the discharge of the remaining patients.

In late October, Ben Curran, the camp manager at Fau II, received the following message:

> Dear Ben,
>   This is just a quick note from TB HELP!
>   Nahun . . . was threatened last night by a TB patient and his friends (big men) about being beaten up if he continued to discharge patients. This man is fierce. He is well [but] does not want to be discharged because he will not get [extra] food in TB when discharged. . . .
>   However, we are to meet this guy and his buddies at the TB center at 12 midday today. Could you please come up and maybe get [a translator]? Otherwise I really think this chap means a lot of trouble.

When Rulester Davis first arrived to administer the nutrition program at Fau III in May, approximately 400 children were registered for intensive, therapeutic feeding — severely malnourished children of less than 70 percent of their normal weight based on height. The list of people enrolled in the supplementary feeding program, which served those more than 70 but less than 80 percent of their normal weight, numbered more than 1,200.

The therapeutic feeding program had become obsolete by the end of the rainy season. Nor was there any need for supplemental feeding: A campwide survey undertaken in early November found that not a single person in camp was below 80 percent normal weight. A very pleased Rulester Davis was thus able to close down the feeding programs altogether at Fau III before she left in November.

By now, all the Western relief workers who had been present from December 1984 to April 1985 were gone. Those who had witnessed the suffering and the death and the starving children of the emergency could not stay to see the final outcome of their own initial efforts. Those workers would remember the camps as a place of despair where the only movement was the morning ritual of carrying out the dead to be buried. It seemed unfair that they should not see the full transformation of the famine camps into communities so full of life and hope.

Flowers blooming at Fau? The thought would have been absurd only a few months ago. The refugees organizing soccer and volleyball games? Schools and adult literacy classes? Laughing and singing? Fat babies and frisbee throwing? At *Fau*? Ridiculous. Yet once the rains dried up in October and the weather turned cooler, this was an accurate portrait of life at Fau.

In late September one day, I was walking towards the clinic at Fau III with the lab technician I had trained months earlier. Suddenly a woman ran up to me and kissed my hand and then disappeared before I had time to react. It was the same woman who had begged me to give her a drink of water from my canteen back in the days when several thousand people had sat in the sun with no tents yet set up for shelter. I wanted to run after her now just to ask if she'd been getting along okay. She had been through so much. They had all been through so much.

At Fau II in October, I recognized one of the boys playing soccer. I recognized him because he had only one eye. Otherwise I would never have known him; it was the boy whose picture I had taken months earlier at the feeding center. He was well now, and strong.

Still, not everyone at Fau was well and happy. In September, after a three-month absence from Fau I, I walked through the camp and all the children followed me as usual. But at the last tent, Hanah's tent, no little girl came running out with her hands above her head. Hanah's mother, who had been standing outside, saw me and slowly shook her head. Then she went inside the tent and closed the canvas flap that served as a door.

Doctors tending the irc clinics noticed that while the numbers of people coming in for physical illnesses were decreasing, more and more people were showing signs of psychological illnesses. Hysteria was becoming common among the refugee women; often women physically well were brought into the clinic unable to move their arms or legs. Women, men, and sometimes even children were carried in feigning unconsciousness and broke into tears upon prodding. That psychological illness among the refugees should become commonplace was not surprising. In the three Fau camps, it would be difficult to find any mother or father who had not lost a child in the past year; it would be hard to find a child who had not lost a brother or sister.

Patient at Fau II feeding center. This patient eventually recovered and became one of the camp's star soccer players.

From October to the end of the year, however, life at Fau really could be described as pleasant. In the daytime, the relief workers felt as if they were an integral part of the refugee community. The clinics were busy, but the doctors and nurses now had the time to really involve themselves in training workers from the camp. This was a challenge because of the language barrier, but several of the relief workers had learned enough Tigrenia to carry on simple conversations.

The emphasis now was away from curative medicine and towards preventative and public health. This brought the relief workers out of the clinics and into the community. The refugees responded, and real friendships developed now. Bonds stronger than ever formed between the relief workers and the refugees.

While walking through Fau III one day in October, I was stopped by a refugee lady and invited into her tent. Inside were two other ladies who appeared to be of middle age, two older men, and several children of all sizes running in and out. They prepared for me a serving of a kind of thick soup made from wheat grains, oil, and water. The flavor was unpleasant, but I smiled as it went down—I was so touched that they should give to me of their poor rations. They spoke no English, and I spoke but little Tigrenia, but we got on well just the same. After nine months of living at one or the other of the three Fau camps, this was the first time I had ever been invited into a refugee's tent to visit. My hostess' name was Goay Gabrehewit. I returned to her tent occasionally; one day I brought along an interpreter, and Goay told me her whole life's story.

Also at Fau III, another refugee endeared himself to many of the relief workers—and exasperated many others. This was Marissa, a 12-year-old Ethiopian Dennis the Menace. He spent his days peeking into windows of the relief workers' living quarters, hoping to be invited in, but mostly being chased away. He hid around corners when the frisbee was being thrown around. Then he darted for the frisbee when he got the chance, grabbed it, and ran away—only to be chased down and have his ears boxed. He once jumped onto the back of a moving pick-up truck being driven by sanitarian Flemming Scheutz. Flemming jumped out and chased him and gave him a solid spanking. Yet when Flemming left camp at the expiration of his contract, Marissa cried.

And what of Nagassy at Fau I? In July, REST had located his father in Gedaref town and brought him to Fau I. At the reunion, Nagassy had cried like a baby, and yet when his father suggested they return to Gedaref, Nagassy pleaded for them to remain at Fau—he couldn't bear to leave his foreign friends at the hospital. The father had lost his wife, his daughter, and a son at Tuklebab; now he would stay with his only remaining son at Fau I.

By November Nagassy no longer worked at the hospital. The
REST had negotiated with IRC to bring in new workers for unskilled
jobs every three months in order to more evenly distribute money from
the salaries. Nagassy still came around the hospital, but he didn't
really have any close friends among the relief workers anymore; they
were all new now and didn't remember him from the early days.

At Fau I and Fau II, the camps were quiet at night, as if the
refugees were afraid to give voice to their most desperate hopes. The
white tents billowed up like hundreds of ghosts against the black sky.
The relief worker walking through camp at night felt like an intruder.
None of the refugees took notice, not even the children. It was as if
the nighttime was their time — their own private quartering for se-
questered reflections. Here and there a small group of children danced
or sang, but quiet prevailed. The families sat outside, gathered
around the embers of the cooking fires and talked quietly among
themselves. The nighttime was their time to remember the pain of the
past, and to hope, to hunger, for the day they might return home,
happy and at peace.

Each camp had its own personality, however, and the nights at
Fau III took the opposite turn. In September and October, bonfires
dotted the camp at night, and the refugees gathered around, dancing
and singing. Songs of home! They were cocksure of going home
soon, and they wanted to celebrate. They were boisterous and
joyous. Homemade beer, made from dates, contributed to the heady
mood. Many of the Fau III relief workers attended these spontaneous
gatherings and, after a couple of cups of the homemade beer, often
attempted to join the circle of dancers. Relief worker attempts to perform the traditional Tigrenia dances never failed to be comical, no
matter how serious the effort, and usually sent the refugee children
rolling on the ground with laughter.

The REST took advantage of the positive morale at Fau III in early
November and organized these impromptu gatherings so that instead of several small parties throughout the camp, one big bonfire
burned — one in each camp section, A through F, on successive nights
of the week. The REST brought in uniformed musicians from Gedaref
town and a troupe of TPLF dancers and singers. Homemade beer was
still served, but the parties had lost much of their spontaneity. After
the bonfire was built and a sufficient number of refugees had gathered
around, the singing and dancing were preceded by several long,

droning political speeches made by REST and TPLF leaders. At the end of each speech the refugees were led to cheer in unison such slogans as "Long live Tigre!" or "Fight on to victory!" or "Death to the enemy!" or "Freedom for our people!" Once the singing and dancing began, each song was followed by one of these slogans and a fist raised in the air. If the slogan wasn't shouted loud enough, the refugees were exhorted to repeat it until it was sufficiently loud and enthusiastic.

The refugees did enjoy these REST-organized gatherings. After all, it was the only entertainment they had experienced in more than a year of suffering and desolation. Upwards of 500 people would attend the parties, which lasted well past midnight. The relief workers continued to attend occasionally although they were often subjected to the embarrassment of formally being seated on folding chairs in a prominent spot while everyone else was standing.

One night in December, Scott Dethloff and I brought our guitars into camp. The REST party was being held way down in section F, so we stopped at a tent in section C where Marissa's family lived. When we began playing and singing a crowd of about 18 people quickly gathered around. It was the first time any relief workers had done something like this; it was something I'd wanted to do for a long time. The refugees were thrilled and delighted.

We played several ballads and rock 'n' roll tunes that were completely lost on the refugees, who tried to clap along with a rhythm in their own distinctive meter. They were more excited about our being there and performing than about actually listening to us. Nevertheless, they applauded wholeheartedly at the conclusion of every song, and there was no raising of the clenched fists.

By and by, we put down our guitars, and the refugees began singing and dancing to their own music. A larger crowd of perhaps 40 people had gathered by now, and the entertainment was marvelous. They sang traditional folksongs that we had never heard before, some involving call-and-response from three separate groups of singers and some with very complicated rhythm patterns. Everyone joined in; even the smallest children knew these songs by heart. They performed unusual dances also: One, called "Aerope," involved the refugees squatting down and holding onto their knees while hopping about like frogs.

The merriment of the party was reminiscent of similar gatherings held in the early autumn, before REST began their more organized events. The air was crisper now at night, and most of the refugees wore long shawls to keep warm.

Suddenly two young men approached the group, one of them obviously intoxicated. Both of them began to scold the group; the more intoxicated one berated them angrily.

Later I learned from one of our translators who was present and from Kristine Coan, a relief worker who was also present and who spoke fairly fluent Tigrenia, that these two individuals were REST members. They were incensed at a group's gathering without REST's permission, especially while a REST-sponsored event was being conducted elsewhere in camp. They were further incensed that the people here were singing traditional songs instead of "revolutionary" songs.

The two REST members demanded to know who had organized the party. A Tigrean priest addressed them apologetically and told them that it was the IRC foreigners who had started it all. The REST members were obviously taken aback at this and, seeing the white faces in the crowd for the first time, lowered their harangue a notch in tone. They concluded by ordering everyone to disperse immediately and go home.

Most of the refugees had already snuck away into the darkness. Those remaining now glanced sheepishly at each other and shuffled off to their tents. It was interesting to see how the priest and a shamagali present, both older men representing the traditional positions of power in the village, yielded to the authority of the REST members without argument or a word in defense of the people. They whispered to themselves and walked off meekly the same as the others.

Certainly the organization, REST, had accomplished much for the people of Tigre. For the best of REST's leaders, the advancement of the welfare of their people is the highest objective for which to strive. But, fed by the idea that the organization knows better the needs of the people than the people themselves, some lesser cadres become less inclined to serve the people than to compel their obedience. The concentration of power in the organization becomes more important than the pursuit of its goals. Thus from the seeds of good intentions grows authoritarianism.

Surely the legitimacy of any civilized political organization must be based on respect for and support from the people. All too often in this world countries are ruled and people are governed by brutish street gangs — terrorist groups which derive their power from intimidation, coercion, and fear. Far too many people in this world live their lives in fear — of violence, of arbitrary arrest and imprisonment, of someone who might be listening or watching.

The REST and the TPLF gained their base of power through efforts to resist the oppression of the government of Addis Ababa but if the cost of liberation is loss of tradition, loss of culture, and loss of freedom, then the cost is very dear indeed. If village families are not allowed to gather and express themselves in dance and song, if spontaneity is suppressed, if the only speech permitted is the mindless repetition of slogans of allegiance to the revolution, then the leaders of the revolution would seem no less odious than the current governing oppressors.

Aside from this particular incident, however, and some minor grumblings about the taxes REST extracted from camp workers on the IRC payroll, there was no apparent tension between REST and the camp people. Many of the refugees at Fau, in fact, were vehement and enthusiastic supporters of REST. One thing was evident: REST compelled their complete obedience.

The anniversay of the opening of Fau, December 12, came and went without notice. There was no good reason to recall the horrors of a year ago. The still total dependence on outside assistance for survival continued to be a dismaying fact of life. Yet there was life here now, and a growing confidence of a better future.

A year ago, among these tents lurked only death and despair. Now these had been replaced by vigor and hope. The refugees had found strength in the depth of their souls. And they had survived through the assistance of an outside world whose compassion had been touched and who had responded so willingly that it seemed there might yet be hope for the redemption of mankind.

The International Rescue Committee was undoubtedly the most responsible for the changing circumstances at Fau. Other Western agencies, GOAL, CARE, and the YMCA, sent personnel and material support, but their operations did not fully begin until May. Public Health International and a Japanese group, RKK, began full operations later still. Only IRC was prepared to offer assistance when it was most needed, when the situation was the most volatile. Its very willingness to go into an unpredictable emergency saved thousands of lives. Though it took several months for its programs to function optimally, the effects of its efforts were felt immediately. Any shortcomings had their roots not in the organization but in the nature of the emergency.

That the quality of life in the camps had improved dramatically was indisputable. Statistics from Public Health International, a public health and sanitation agency operating under the umbrella of IRC, indicated that drinking water chlorination was satisfactory in up to 99 percent of frequent random testing — a remarkable achievement in a refugee camp setting. Through improved cleanliness and more effective use of insecticides, the flies never again became the nuisance they had been a year earlier. Clotheslines were in constant use. Malnutrition was nonexistent. The trees planted at Fau I had grown more than two feet during the rainy season. And the refugees were cheerful and happy.

There were only 14 full-time IRC staff members remaining at Fau at year's end. Most of them would be going home in the next few months, and there were no plans to replace them. The programs in place were run largely by the refugees themselves. The goal now was to maintain the programs unchanged until the refugees went home and the camps were closed.

There had been a general improvement in most of the famine-affected areas of Africa over the past year. The massive relief effort had been effective. In Ethiopia, in the Sudan, assistance was even getting through to Chad. Great progress had been achieved in all the refugee camps in eastern Sudan, even at Wad Kowli; but at Fau, the achievements were the most evident and the most dramatic.

The mortality rates at Fau for the final three months of 1985 were as follows: October, 10.3 deaths per 10,000 population; November, 6.2/10,000; and December, 5.4/10,000. Although no one had any hard data to back up the assertion, it was generally held that the "normal" mortality rate for a village in Tigre was 9–10/10,000 population per month. Thus in the 12 months of the camps' existence, a normal level of health had finally been achieved at Fau.

In late November, I found a one-page document on the common dining room table at the Fau II compound. It read as follows:

MESSAGE TO THE AMERICAN PEOPLE

From the Shamagalis (Elders) of Fau II Ethiopian Refugee Camp

Thanks to the American people for their contributions. Now we are in good health. Now and forever, don't forget us. We don't forget you. Before we came here, we are on the way to death. But now we are alive. Don't forget us and we don't forget you, you are good.

. . . We are happy with these American people that you send us.

We came from Tigre to here. On the way, 27 are dead by the plane, and 57 are severely wounded. . . . This happened while we are eating lunch. We had no weapons, just we have only our walking sticks. This happened near Sherallo, after 12 days of journey from our village in Tigre.

We need your prayers from the American church to keep us from this bad situation now in Ethiopia. We also need clothes or cloth to make our clothes. But even if we don't get, we are happy for the hope. Hence, hereafter, and in the future, we will have good hope.

X. Going Home at Last

On December 15, about 200 new refugees arrived at Fau III on COR transport. These were Tigreans who had recently crossed the border into the Sudan near the town of Damazin in the Southern Region. They had escaped from a relocation center in southern Ethiopia after being forced there from their homes in Tigre by Ethiopian government troops.

In the autumn of 1984, as the famine was reaching emergency proportions, the Ethiopian government in Addis Ababa had decided to create new relocation centers in the southern and western provinces for the starving inhabitants of the northern highlands— Tigre and Wollo provinces. The idea held merit: famine victims would be removed from densely populated areas of rocky, overcultivated, overgrazed, depleted soil and limited access and be deposited in areas of low population density, lush vegetation and fertile soil, and easy accessibility.

The plan was also ambitious, perhaps overly so: one and one-half million famine victims were to be relocated within 12 months at an estimated cost of about double the country's annual budget. Nevertheless, the program was undertaken and as early as January 1985, with the help of 12 Soviet-built Antonov cargo aircraft and more than 300 Soviet supplied trucks, 120,000 persons had already been relocated. By January 1986, more than half a million persons had been relocated.

From the start, the program was controversial. Some saw it as a possible long-term solution to the underlying long-term problem. Blaine Harden of the *Washington Post* reported:

> Foreign agricultural experts here say the drought-seared land has been ruined, probably for decades, by deforestation, erosion, overpopulation, and destructive farm practices. There is no way, these specialists say, that the highlands can feed the 7 million or so people who now live there. [*Washington Post*, 3 January 1985.]

In the same article, Alan Court of UNICEF declared, "the peasants who are being moved to the south are being fed . . . and soon they will be able to grow their own food."

Many Tigreans, on the other hand, especially REST and TPLF spokesmen, denounced the relocation program as a military attempt to depopulate areas of resistance. The newly created villages, under strict military guard, were constructed because of political, not humanitarian concerns. As such, they were reminiscent of the agrovilles or "strategic hamlets" that the South Vietnamese leader, Ngo Dinh Diem, had tried unsuccessfully to maintain during the Vietnam War.

In fact, had the relocation program proceeded on a completely voluntary basis as the Ethiopian government had promised, no justifiable complaints could have been leveled against it. Many inhabitants of the relocation centers, however, had been forced to leave their homes against their wishes and had been shipped to the centers in a manner that very much resembled that of a military operation:

> Survival International, a British organization, said people are being forced at gunpoint into airplanes and vehicles and transported in such crowded conditions that many die before reaching their destinations. [*Africa Report* **31** no. 1 (January/ February 1986). Copyright ©1986 by the African-American Institute. Reprinted by permission of *Africa Report*.]

The controversy reached its peak on 3 December 1985 when the Ethiopian government expelled the French relief organization, Médecins Sans Frontiers, for publicly charging that between 50,000 and 100,000 famine victims had died as a result of being transferred forcibly to the south. The French agency had the indomitability to say publicly what other relief organizations would say only anonymously.

Undoubtedly, humanitarian concerns were basic to the conception of the relocation program. That the program would also enhance government military and political strength in the rebellious areas added immensely to its appeal within government circles. The program was given priority, and as so often happens in programs for the people but not of the people, overzealous cadres misused their authority. The program had merit, but in the end a program borne of good intentions was used as an instrument to exercise force and subjugation.

By March of 1986, as many as 1,500 escapees of the relocation centers had made their way into the Sudan at Damazin. Many of these were moved by COR to refugee camps in the Eastern Region, but no more were to come to Fau after December.

Those relocation center escapees who did come to Fau caused much excitement among the refugees, for they carried with them firsthand accounts of conditions back in Tigre. Their descriptions were bittersweet.

Lagasse Terfe, one of those who had come to Fau from Damazin, told me that, yes, it had rained in Tigre; in fact, it had been an excellent rainy season. But there hadn't been enough seed to plant the fields, most of the oxen for plowing had died the year before, also many of the farmers had died and many had abandoned their fields to come to the Sudan. As a result of all these factors, some areas of Tigre had yielded but poor harvests and food was far from plentiful. Still, the problems were nothing like those of last year. No one was starving; there was no danger of famine in the coming year.

Back in January of 1985, even as the first lorries were transferring their cargoes of human misery from Tuklebab to Fau, officials from both COR and REST had told relief workers that the refugees probably would remain at Fau only "a few months." During the first several weeks and indeed throughout the remainder of the year, rumors persisted of an impending repatriation of the refugees back to Tigre. One reason why the plans for partial repatriation in May had been met with such skepticism by the relief workers then was that several such reports in the preceding months had proven to be false.

Continued talk of repatriation slowed down during the rainy season when movement was impossible, but once the weather turned dry, circulation of the rumors picked up again. With the improved health status in the camps and reports of a fair harvesting season in Tigre, the rumors were much more credible than before. As the year drew to a close, feelings of expectation in the camps grew stronger. The refugees were fit and made no secret of their desire to return home. They waited only for the word from REST.

In mid–January REST started registering people to return to Tigre. At about the same time, several more new refugees began trickling into the Fau camps: These were men coming from Tigre to collect their families to go back home. The population at Fau at the end of the year had been approximately 21,300; at mid–February the population had increased to 23,500. No one doubted that the long-awaited repatriation was imminent. The camps buzzed with excitement.

The IRC, UNHCR, and other relief agencies worked with COR and REST to plan the repatriation. The first people to go back would be those living at the Wad Kowli camp near the border. Of the 39,000 people at Wad Kowli, 30,000 were expected to repatriate. Those remaining would eventually be relocated to a more accessible location.

After repatriation from Wad Kowli was complete, a section of that camp would be set aside as a staging area for people coming from Fau and from other refugee camps in the Eastern Region. Those repatriating from Fau would journey the same way they had first arrived — on the backs of Bedford lorry trucks.

The refugees would travel three hours from Fau to Tawawa refugee camp outside of Gedaref town, where they could refresh themselves with clean water provided by IRC sanitation before continuing on the further four hours to Wad Kowli. After a one- or two-night rest at the Wad Kowli staging site, the refugees would resume their journey back to their villages on foot. For some, the trek would take only a few days; for others it would take weeks. For all of them the final destination would be home at last.

By now all the green of the rainy season had turned to brown. The swaying grasses of three months earlier had become stiff, yellow reeds rustling in the dry wind. The clouds had disappeared from the sky and a hint of dust scented the air.

With the tall dry grass as relief, the horizon seemed less formidable than it had a year ago. Still, the flatness of the land played tricks with one's depth perception. A grazing camel appeared to be only about a hundred yards away when in fact it was nearly half a mile from the observer. The headlights of a truck approaching camp at night seemed to take forever to arrive.

So clear was the sky at night that it became three dimensional. Some stars appeared farther away than others, and satellites regularly crossed in front of the stars in silent flight. Meteor showers were common; nearer falling stars flashed green or red before streaking to extinction. Pleiades was never clearer or more beautiful. Halley's Comet, barely visible, called to mind the prophecy of Nostradamus that in the year of the comet a great famine would touch all the world.

January passed quickly. The usual medical and sanitation work in the camps continued; in addition, IRC prepared first aid kits and set up extra water tanks at Tawawa in anticipation of repatriation.

Approximately 6,000 people were expected to elect to remain at Fau rather than repatriate. These included the TB patients who had not completed their 12-month treatment; others too debilitated, sick, or otherwise physically unfit to make the arduous journey; and some who had lost their homes or who felt they had nothing to return to in Tigre. Of special concern to IRC staff was the inevitable psychological trauma to be experienced by those remaining. While for most of the refugees, the long nightmare was coming to an end, there were others for whom the idea of continuing indefinitely this dismal existence would only now be fully apprehended.

On 3 February 1986, about 500 refugees departed from Wad Kowli on foot, heading for villages in Tigre. The repatriation had begun. For nearly a quarter of a million Tigrean famine victims who had fled into the Sudan in search of survival in the fall and winter of 1984, the untold suffering and sorrow would soon be only a memory.

At Fau, the nightly celebrations ceased and nervous anticipation set in. The waiting lasted for three weeks. Then, on the morning of February 25, 18 Bedford lorries appeared at Fau I. The local Sudanese police joined REST and COR in overseeing their loading. While the sun was still low in the sky and before the daytime heat had conquered the coolness of the night, the lorries, one by one and each carrying 50 refugees, labored onto the bumpy washboard road that led out of camp. Twenty minutes later they had passed by Fau II within 50 yards

of the tents there. The refugees at Fau II cheered as they saw the lorries roll by, and the children jumped up and down in excitement.
Their friends were going home, and they knew that they would be
soon to follow.

Well before noon, the lorries pulled off the main tarmac road
and onto the dirt road that led to Tawawa camp. The sanitation
workers had set up the water and rest station several hundred yards
from Tawawa to keep that camp's inhabitants from interfering with
the operation. Water containers were passed around, and several of
the refugees poured the contents of foil ORS packets into the water — a
practice they had learned at Fau to prevent dehydration. At the rest
stop most of the refugees remained on the lorries, so impatient were
they to resume their journey. They seemed so careless and comfortable that one might have thought they were simply out for an afternoon picnic.

After half an hour, the lorries pulled back onto the tarmac road,
and then after only a quarter of a mile onto another dirt road that
wound around Gedaref town, past a series of stinking garbage heaps,
through the Muslim cemetery on the outskirts of town, eventually
turning to follow the Atbara River through tiny Sudanese villages
and several villages of Nigerian settlers. Finally, just as the landscape
turned from flat to hilly and the vegetation from sparse to tropical,
the lorries stopped at the refugee camp of Wad Kowli, only seven
miles from the Ethiopian border.

I was at the Tawawa water station that day and had driven on
out ahead of the refugees to Wad Kowli. The camp organization here
was quite different from the other refugee camps in the Eastern
Region; the tents were not laid out in rows, nor arranged in squares
or rectangular sections. Here the camp had evolved spontaneously
as the refugees migrated in. It sprawled over a wide area along the
eastern bank of the Atbara River. Tents and straw huts tended to
cluster together, and the inhabitants of each cluster of dwellings were
generally from a particular village or district of Tigre. In fact, the
camp was divided into 28 separate "villages": here was Adua, beyond
was Gwaro, nearer the river was Maychew and Sherallo, up on the
hill was Axum, and farther down at the southern end were Enticho
and Nadir.

The first 900 returnees from Fau arrived at Wad Kowli at mid-
afternoon. They climbed down from the lorries and milled about the

straw and wooden pole shelters that had been constructed for them. Dry sugar biscuits were distributed by REST and the cooking fires were started.

Thirteen thousand people had repatriated from Wad Kowli in the past three weeks; further repatriation from Wad Kowli had been postponed to allow returning refugees from other camps the advantage of movement during the dry season.

In the late afternoon I took a walk through Wad Kowli and then circled around to the staging area on the northern edge of camp. I was hoping to recognize some of the Fau refugees there. As I loitered about the site I saw a few faintly familiar faces, and several of the refugees waved and shouted "Salaam!" in recognition of me. Many were busy rearranging their bundles, others talked carelessly among themselves, and the inevitable soccer ball occupied an entire legion of kids.

Many of the Fau refugees had wandered into Wad Kowli camp, and some residents of Wad Kowli had walked up to the staging area. Women shrieked in joyful recognition of family and neighbors from whom they had been separated for more than a year. They kissed each other on both cheeks several times in the traditional Ethiopian greeting for close friends and relatives.

Walking about as I was without any real purpose, I again had a vague feeling of being an outsider, an intruder into private affairs. But the beaming faces and the hopeful smiles around me produced a quiet sense of happiness in my own heart: I had been witness to the worst of their pain and sorrow, and now I felt privileged to be present at their deliverance.

I lingered near the onion skin temporary water tanks for about 15 minutes, watching the refugees. I wondered what would they find upon their return and half wished I could accompany them. It was evident here watching them that it was all over now, the nightmare had finally ended, they were going home.

The sun was fast sinking, and it was time for me to walk across the bridge over the river to the IRC compound. I had taken about a dozen steps in that direction when I was stopped by a voice. "Jim! Jim!"

There, tugging at my shirttail, all smiles and bright eyes as always, stood Nagassy. In a gesture of respect, he kissed my hand, and then, pointing towards the forests to the east, he said excitedly in

English, "Home! My home!" Then he reached into his little bag and pulled out the photograph of me that I had given him long ago.

In the morning, just as the first grey streaks of dawn lightened the eastern skies, the refugees, in groups of 20 to 50, slowly departed from the staging area, walking towards the dawn. Leading the groups were the men with walking sticks in hand, white shawls pulled over their shoulders, and pride of purpose on their faces. The women strapped sleeping babies to their backs and followed. The children, still too sleepy to cause much commotion, marched along quietly. In a short while, the refugees from Fau had disappeared into the hills and forests leading into Tigre. Very few turned to look back.

Conclusion

Repatriation from Fau proceeded swiftly. The last truckload of returnees left Fau III on March 16. All but approximately 5,600 of the original Fau refugees had returned to their homes.

In March, COR had planned to transfer those refugees left behind at Fau to Safawa, a camp 35 miles west of Wad Kowli. Wad Kowli itself was dismantled in April and the remaining refugees there moved to Safawa. The transfer of the Fau refugees was not accomplished until nearly another year had passed, however, because of intragovernmental disputes over who would control the land at the Fau sites once the refugees were gone.

In February 1987, REST announced plans for a final repatriation of famine victims from eastern Sudan to Tigre. Nine hundred refugees from Fau repatriated to Tigre in February and March. Then, on 20 March 1987, the remaining 4,535 Fau refugees were transferred to Safawa and the Fau camps were completely dismantled.

The Fau sites were washed with rain from June to September of 1987. All the remaining vestiges of camp life — the mounds of straw where once stood the IRC clinics, the blackened earth where once were stored thousands of burlap bags of charcoal in the COR storage tent, the dug-out earthen walls that the refugees had built at each tent to protect the cooking fires from the wind, the rotting sandal that had slipped off someone's foot in the rush to board the repatriation lorry — all of these traces were lost, washed away by the rains. At the southeast corner of each camp where hundreds of mounds of earth once marked the fate of so many of the famine's victims, only a few dozen graves had still been visible. These too disappeared with the rains. Once the standing water drained and the tall grasses again turned to brown, the sites of Fau II and Fau III could no longer be located with certainty: they had become indistinguishable from the surrounding dusty landscape. But at Fau I, the 1,000 acacia and eucalyptus trees planted in that terrible spring of 1985 still stand testament, clustered alone in the Sudanese desert, the only remaining visible sign of the struggle for life at Fau.

Goay Gabrehewit bribed her way past COR officials when the repatriation trucks stopped at Tawawa camp. She made her way into Gedaref town, found her sister, and now lives relatively comfortably with her children and her sister's family in a compound of four huts. They have electric lighting, a refrigerator, and are contemplating the purchase of a television set.

Kasai Maskal returned to Tigre during the February and March repatriations of 1986. Before he left, he told me he planned to return to Axum to resume his studies for the priesthood.

Zorai Abraha returned to Tigre in May 1985 to work in the fields of his parents' farm. He returned to Fau in January 1986, and in February both he and Ngistie repatriated. They will attempt, like so many others, to put the tragedy behind them and reconstruct their lives.

The rains returned again to Ethiopia in 1986. Once again, the victims of the Great Famine were leading normal lives. But it should be remembered that normal lives for so many of these people meant lives of hunger, poverty, and fear of political violence.

Nor should it be forgotten that famine haunts this land like an evil spectre awaiting the next drought. And drought did occur again, in 1987. By December of that year, food shortages had become so severe that another mass migration of Ethiopians into the Sudan appeared imminent. The *Sudan Times* reported that 7,000 refugees had entered the Sudan during the last week of November. A situation report dated 3 December 1987 for Save the Children's Fund, U.K., stated, "It seems likely that there will be a substantial influx of refugees into eastern Sudan. . . . The most likely number seems to be 200,000 to 300,000. . . ."

Several factors, however, combined to prevent the expected migration. First, and most important, the Sudanese government made clear its unwillingness to allow more refugees in. Sayed Hassan Attiya, Commissioner for Refugees, stated in the October 30 edition of the *Sudan Times*, "Sudan has exhausted its capacity for absorbing more refugees.... There is no obligation on Sudan to protect ... people coming here because of famine." The UNHCR and the relief agencies were forbidden to establish contingency operations and were forbidden to plan or even discuss the situation with COR. To accentuate its stated position, the Sudanese government in late 1987 stationed additional military troops along the Ethiopian border.

Second, cross-border feeding operations coordinated by Lutheran World Relief were expanded. Substantial shipments of food had been trucked overland from the Sudan since 1985 with logistical support from the International Committee of the Red Cross and with funding from the United States and West European governments. In early 1988, the United States Agency for International Development greatly increased its support for the program. More food was made available to REST and the TPLF and to the rebel groups in Eritrea for distribution.

Finally, unlike three years earlier, the 45 foreign and domestic relief agencies inside Ethiopia were well-prepared for such a crisis. They had learned how to handle the Ethiopian ports and transportation system. More important, they had devised a coordinated plan to avoid the migration of entire families and villages. The plan called for heads of families to report to food centers once each month for a four-week supply of food. Distribution in this fashion began in August, after it had become clear that the 1987 harvest had failed. A United Nations airlift of food supplies augmented the distribution plan during the winter of 1987–88.

With effective feeding operations underway, containment of the crisis seemed assured. Then, in the spring of 1988, the ongoing military conflicts escalated. In late February, the TPLF captured the Tigrean capital of Makele. By the end of March, they had taken Axum and Adua and had driven the Ethiopian army out of Tigre Province altogether. At the same time, the government army was suffering similarly humiliating defeats at the hands of rebels in Eritrea. In the villages, the rebel victories resulted in disruption of the relief effort, renewed food shortages, and increased hardships.

In response to the military defeats, Ethiopia's President Mengistu ordered the closure of all roads into and out of Tigre. Although the TPLF allowed the relief workers to carry out operations, supplies dwindled and the food supply effort ground to a near halt. Then, on April 6, 1988, Mengistu ordered all foreign relief organizations, including the Red Cross and Catholic Relief Services, to withdraw their

personnel from Tigre and Eritrea, suspending operations altogether.
The indigenous relief agencies, the Ethiopian Red Cross, the Ethiopian Catholic Secretariat, the Orthodox Church, and Mekkonen
Jesus, were similarly forbidden to operate in the northern provinces.
The people of Tigre now had practically no communication with the
outside world. Their daily struggles against hunger were hidden
behind the shadows of war.

As the Sudanese border to the west closed to migration, and relief supplies from the south ceased completely, silent walls of hunger
and suffering encircled the victims of the latest drought. And the
story disappeared from newspapers as foreign journalists were forbidden to enter the war zones. The international community, so com-
passionate a few years earlier, seemed largely indifferent, as if the
world had grown tired of hearing about Ethiopia's problems.

The rains that fell then, in the summer of 1988, averted what
would certainly have been a disaster of great magnitude. A respite
of normalcy returned to village life. Food again became available in
the markets. Government soldiers were gone from the towns. The
latest crisis had passed.

But the rains were poor again in 1989. Although other areas of
Ethiopia received heavy rainfall, large areas of Tigre Province remain dry.

An official of USAID recently told the author:

These reports of drought were current through the end of July.
Since then, it has rained, but amounts are 75% of normal. There
are food shortages.

The risk area is the western half of Tigre Province; in the east,
the situation is relatively good. We rely mainly on satellite images
for weather and crop information, especially now that there is no
government presence in the area. Information from the guerrillas
is not reliable. The rains are late however; they should have been
well underway by June.

As you may know, the guerrillas overran Tigre last spring....
This has caused some hardships due to a reduced amount of
money in circulation. Most exchanges are done through barter.

Trying to get information on the feeding centers has been
difficult. The TPLF is bringing in some food from the Sudan
through an area called Shire near the border. Yes, Lutheran World
Relief was overseeing these operations, but I can't comment on
their present status....

There have been few reports so far of cross-border migration into the Sudan; 50 to 100 people are reportedly coming per week — nothing of that sort which occurred in 1984 and 1985. This has been of some surprise to us. Some internal migration has occurred toward the south, to government-controlled areas. . . .

Ethiopia's President Mengistu survived an army mutiny and coup attempt in May 1989, but his government was badly weakened. The Ethiopian economy never recovered from the 1984–85 collapse, the wars in Eritrea and Tigre are all but lost, and the Soviet Union is withdrawing its military support at the same time that it is pressing for payments on past weapons debts.

Because of these economic, military, and political failures, Mengistu has been forced to reshape his government's posture. He has made friendly overtures to the United States, and has met with former President Jimmy Carter and with the late Congressman Mickey Leland. He has assented to a withdrawal of the 3,000 Cuban troops stationed in Ethiopia, and he has begun peace negotiations with his nemesis, the Eritrean People's Liberation Front. He is negotiating with the International Committee of the Red Cross about the possible resumption of relief operations in the northern provinces. According to a visitor returned from Ethiopia in September 1989, he has even loosened control of domestic life in Addis Ababa, allowing curfews to go unenforced and permitting farmers to sell fruits and vegetables in open markets instead of through the government-owned stores.

What the outcome of Mengistu's maneuvers will be, no one can say. But while the international community focuses its attention on the political positioning in Addis Ababa, hunger and indigence continue to afflict the villages of Tigre Province.

For the villagers of Tigre the winter of 1989–90 was a time of privation. The rainy season summer months loom as a time of anxiety. The anguish and despair of five years ago have not been forgotten. Those who lived at Fau during those dreadful times will remember the misery and death, but they will also recall the help they received there and the hope they regained. And they will recall that at Fau they discovered the inner strength that can only be educed from grief — the strength they will need to face a future so uncertain and so ominous.

Appendix : Mortality Rates

Record keeping was spotty at Fau from January to September 1985. Sometimes deaths were reported as estimated rates (sometimes per day, sometimes per month) rather than as total number of deaths, and sometimes figures from one or the other Fau camps were missing altogether. Sometimes figures from two different sources for the same camp for the same month conflicted. Population figures were also often only estimations. Even where records were kept carefully, some deaths went unreported and were therefore not recorded. The figures quoted in the book are based on calculations using the only records available, faulty as they may be.

Before September, the most carefully collected data were compiled in the first month, January 1985. This is the only month where figures are available for total population and for total number of deaths for all three camps.

Even January's data have to be manipulated, though, because movement of refugees into the camps meant the populations differed from the first of the month to the last of the month. An average population is therefore calculated that assumes that refugees arrived each day at camp in equal numbers. Mortality rates must then be divided by the number of days the camp was in existence and then multiplied by 31 days to obtain the rates for January.

The calculations for determining mortality rate at Fau for January are given below:

	Pop. at First of Month		Pop. at Last of Month		Average Pop.
Fau I	9126		8933		9030
Fau II	0	+	13,269	/ 2 =	6635
Fau III	0		13,672		6836
			Total Avg. Pop.		22,501

	Number of Recorded Deaths	Deaths/Avg. Pop.
Fau I	191	0.0212
Fau II	195	0.0294
Fau III	66	0.0097

	Deaths/Avg. Pop. Days Camp Existed in January		Deaths/Avg. Pop. for January
Fau I	0.0212/31		0.0212
Fau II	0.0294/28	× 31 =	0.0326
Fau III	0.0097/ 7		0.0430

Deaths/Avg. Pop. for January × Avg. Pop./Total Avg. Pop.

Fau I	0.0212×9030/22,501 = 0.0085
Fau II	0.0326×6635/22,501 = 0.0096
Fau III	0.0430×6836/22,501 = 0.0130
	0.0311

0.0311×10,000 = 311 Deaths/10,000 Population

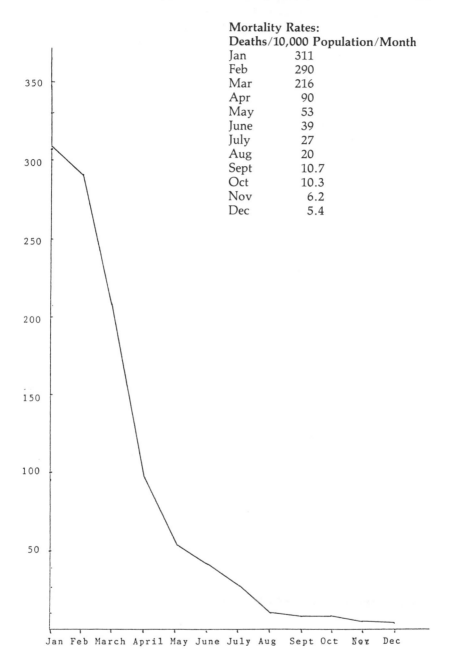

Mortality Rates:
Deaths/10,000 Population/Month

Jan	311
Feb	290
Mar	216
Apr	90
May	53
June	39
July	27
Aug	20
Sept	10.7
Oct	10.3
Nov	6.2
Dec	5.4

Bibliography

Anderson, Jack. "Compassion by Committee." *Washington Post*, 17 January 1985, DC9.

On an inter-governmental agency task force set up to deal with the Ethiopian crisis, Fred Wettering of the National Security Council took the view that aid from the United States should be forthcoming only after the Ethiopian government made strategic political concessions. This proposition was the main obstacle to United States aid to Ethiopia from 1983 to 1984.

Billard, Annick. "Eastern Sudan: Huge Efforts Paying Off." *Refugees* no. 27, pp. 19–28. Geneva: United Nations High Commissioner for Refugees, March 1986.

A review of the UNHCR-assisted programs established in the Sudan in 1985 concluding that medium- and long-term planning have now replaced emergency priorities. Contains a map of the refugee camps and several pairs of photographs contrasting the current rehabilitation to the despair of 12 months earlier.

Cater, Nick. *Sudan: The Roots of Famine.* Oxford: Oxfam, 1986.

Cater details several factors contributing to the Sudan's own famine of 1984–85. The most important: deforestation, export-oriented agricultural policies, and the soaring populations of both humans and livestock settling around boreholes meant as temporary water stops for nomads.

Doresse, Jean. *Ethiopia: Ancient Cities and Temples.* Translated from the French by Elsa Coult. London: Elek; New York: Putnam, 1959. (First published in 1956 as *Au Pays de la Reine de Saba l'Ethiopie Antique et Moderne* by Editions d'Art Albert Guillat et Cie).

A unique book on ancient and mediaeval Ethiopia that illustrates the symbiotic evolution of history and religion. Contains numerous photographs of religious architecture, paintings, sculptures, and engravings. Of

138 Bibliography

special interest are the photographs of the interior of the Cathedral of Axum and the single photograph of the entrance to the Chapel of the Tablet of Moses.

Eldridge, Chris. *Situation Report*. Report for Save the Children's Fund, U.K., 3 December 1987.

Discusses a possible refugee influx of great magnitude into the Sudan as a result of the 1987 60 percent crop failure in Tigre Province.

Frey, Rob. *Monthly Medical Report*. International Rescue Committee program report, January 1985.

The only IRC report until September 1985 that includes comprehensive morbidity and mortality statistics.

————. *Monthly Medical Report*. International Rescue Committee program report, February 1985.

Mortality figures are presented as estimated deaths per 10,000 population per day.

————. *Monthly Medical Report*. International Rescue Committee program report, March 1985.

Includes a recommendation for additional expatriate staff and observations on the tuberculosis problem.

Giorgis, Dowit Wolde. *Red Tears*. Trenton, N.J.: Red Sea, 1989.

A comprehensive account of the famine and the political controversy that swirled around it, written by the one person most competent in the subject, the former Commissioner of the Ethiopian Relief and Rehabilitation Commission. The book is Mr. Giorgis' own confirmation of his international image as a man of compassion caught between a pitiless Ethiopian dictator and a skeptical world community.

Girardet, Edward. "Ethiopia: Hunger Is Not the Only Battle." *Christian Science Monitor*, 4 January 1985.

Discusses how delivery of relief and food supplies in Tigre and Eritrea was hampered by the civil strife in these areas. Includes photograph of Tigreans abandoning the town of Zela Zele in western Tigre Province for the Sudan. (Photograph by Chris Carter, Grassroots International.)

————. "Africa's Immediate Need and Its Longer-Term Prospects." *Christian Science Monitor*, 15 January 1985.

Includes a description of the conditions at Tuklebab with mention of the relocation of the camp's population to El Fau.

Hacket, Kenneth. "Will the Tragedy Be Repeated?" *Africa Report* 29, no. 4, pp. 19–23. African-American Institute, July-August 1984.

The author, senior director of Catholic Relief Services/Africa, argues that famine results not from drought alone, but from drought coupled with absolute poverty. Disturbed by the amount of resources directed to military and security concerns, he suggests that famine will occur unless African governments and the international donor community focus attention on improving infrastructure (roads and ports), public services (health and education), and agricultural production.

Harden, Blaine. "U.S. Airlifts Relief Goods to the Sudan." *Washington Post*, 28 December 1984.

52,000 Ethiopians have entered the Sudan in the past 12 days with at least another 50,000 en route. In response to an emergency appeal from the UNHCR, President Reagan has ordered an airlift of portable water tanks, blankets, tents, and measles vaccines to the Sudan for use at the three new refugee camps at Wad Sharife, Safawa, and Tuklebab.

————. "Ethiopia Presses Resettlement." *Washington Post*, 3 January 1985.

As a long-term solution to the agricultural crisis, the Ethiopian government has relocated 120,000 from drought-afflicted areas in the north to fertile, depopulated areas in the south. The United States has been quick to condemn the resettlement program; some other Western countries and relief agencies believe relocation to be a viable long-term strategy.

Heiden, David. *Medical Activities and Problems Report, Fau III.* International Rescue Committee program report, 31 March 1985.

Discusses expatriate staffing problem, ethnic tensions in camp, and the issue of treatment for tuberculosis.

Interfam Information Project. *Briefing Packet: Famine in the Non-Government Held Areas of Eritrea and Ethiopia, and Refugees in Eastern Sudan.* Khartoum, the Sudan: Interfam, August 1985.

An invaluable booklet containing maps of Eritrea and Tigre provinces and of the border area refugee camps, a description of the resistance movements of Eritrea and Tigre, a list of important officials at COR and UNHCR, and a list of non-governmental agencies operating in the Sudan. Of particular interest is the 7-page summary of the history of Tigre, including the origins of the TPLF, the founding of REST, and a description of the internal REST-operated food supply program at 17 reception centers in western Tigre established in May 1983.

Jones, A.H.M., and Monroe, Elizabeth. *A History of Ethiopia.* London: Oxford University Press 1968. (First published October 1935 under the title *A History of Abyssinia.*)

Beginning with the mythical origins of the Kingdom of Axum and ending with the conflict with Italy in 1935, most of this book is concerned with Ethiopian history prior to the nineteenth century. Especially detailed is the Christian evangelization of the Kingdom of Axum, its contacts with the Roman empire, and its eventual separation from the rest of Christendom by the rise of Islam.

Kapuscinski, Ryszard. *The Emperor.* Orlando, Fla.: Harcourt Brace Jovanovich, 1983. (Originally published as *Cesarz* by Czytelnik, Warsaw; 1978.)

A collection of interviews and recollections from members of the Court of Emperor Haile Selassie. Though the anecdotes ae fascinating, the thread of history is sometimes lost in personal nostalgia. The anonymity of the speakers, moreover, further detracts from a chronology that is unclear.

Menning, Mike. Letter to IRC headquarters, New York, 31 October 1984.

A detailed letter focusing on plans for the three new reception centers at Fau. A long list of concerns is evidence of apprehension of further involvement in the deteriorating situation.

Nickerson, Colin. "Refugees Streaming into Sudan." *Boston Globe,* 17 November 1984.

The first published description of the refugee camp at Tuklebab, written when the camp was only one week in existence.

Novicki, Margaret A. "Interview: Harry Belafonte." *Africa Report* 30 no. 5, pp. 21–36. African-American Institute, September-October 1985.

Belafonte describes the creation of the USA for Africa project. He concludes that short-term crises will continue to unfold until a commitment is made to massive assistance for long-term development.

Ottaway, David B. "Ethiopians Fleeing to Sudan from Ravages of Drought, War." *Washington Post,* 18 March 1983.

Sudanese and international agency officials hold conflicting views on the probability of a mass influx of Ethiopian refugees into the Sudan. Jon Eklund of the International Rescue Committee says that, as a result of reports of refugee migration, IRC will stay on, rather than wind down its activities in the Sudan.

————. "Ethiopia Faces Famine with 'Tens of Thousands' in Danger." *Washington Post,* 18 September 1984.

With villagers from the northern provinces already flooding the towns and food stations, most observers say the latest crop failure ensures a famine of greater magnitude than that of 1973–74. Despite impassioned pleas from Dawit Wolde Giorgis, head of Ethiopia's Relief and Rehabilitation Commission, international assistance has been slow in coming because of "donor fatigue" and a dislike of Ethiopia's Soviet-oriented socialist policies.

_____. "U.S. Helps Ethiopian Rebel Area." *Washington Post,* 14 April 1985.

The United States government, working through the Agency for International Development, has been involved in cross-border relief operations from the Sudan into northern Ethiopia since early 1984 by channeling funds to Lutheran World Relief, Mercy Corps International, and the International Committee of the Red Cross.

Press, Robert M. "Severe Drought Spurs Call for Aid." *Christian Science Monitor,* 3 October 1989.

The 1989 harvests in northern Ethiopia have been erratic with some parts of Tigre Province experiencing almost total crop failure. Because the TPLF now controls all of the province, most aid for Tigre will have to go through the rebel channels from neighboring Sudan.

Randal, Jonathan C. "Instant City in Sudan." *Washington Post,* 2 February 1985.

The major concern at the Wad Kowli refugee camp, population 70,000 since first arrivals appeared December 10, is that the water supply is expected to be exhausted within 10 weeks.

REST Press Release. Relief Society of Tigre, P.O. Box 8078, Khartoum, The Sudan, 22 January 1983.

An appeal for food, clothing, medicine, or cash. REST warns that food supplies are low and that grain stocks are needed to prevent an exodus of refugees into the Sudan.

REST Press Release. Relief Society of Tigre, P.O. Box 8078, Khartoum, The Sudan, 30 November 1984.

REST reports that 25,000 people have entered the Sudan in the past two weeks; 30,000 to 50,000 more are en route. REST accuses the Ethiopian government of withholding food supplies from those above 45 years old and from those who refuse to sign up for resettlement.

REST Press Release. Relief Society of Tigre, P.O. Box 8078, Khartoum, The Sudan, 4 February 1985.

More than 100,000 Tigreans have entered the Sudan, and 2,000 more are arriving each day. REST claims that international assistance to the Ethiopian government does not reach the Tigrean countryside, and that this catastrophe could have been averted if the world community had provided sufficient aid to REST.

Safran, Claire. *Secret Exodus.* Englewood Cliffs, N. J.: Prentice-Hall, 1987.

This book recounts the CIA- and Mossad-run Operation Moses, in which 16,000 Ethiopian Jews (Falashas) were spirited to Israel from Ethiopia via the Sudan in early 1985. In reading of the risks undertaken by United States embassy personnel and of the great effort expended at this and higher levels of the State Department, one cannot help wondering how such attention was given to this small group while a quarter million others starved.

Shepherd, Jack. "The Politics of Food Aid." *Africa Report* 30 no. 2, pp. 51–54. African-American Institute, March-April 1985.

Shepherd criticizes Ethiopia's leader, Lt. Col. Mengistu, for spending $45 million on the tenth anniversary of the Ethiopian revolution in September 1984 and for assigning port priority to ships loaded with supplies for the celebration over those loaded with emergency food. He also criticizes the dilatory American reaction to the Ethiopian crisis — the administration's inadequate response to funding requests from Catholic Relief Services made through the United States Agency for International Development, USAID's decision not to request any food aid for Ethiopia in 1984, and the attempt by the executive branch to attach an amendment calling for military aid to the Nicaraguan Contras to the supplemental appropriations for African aid.

————. "Food Aid: Congress and the White House at Odds." *Africa Report* 30 no. 3, pp. 25–28. African-American Institute, May-June 1985.

The White House, according to Shepherd, supports short-term emergency relief aid, but opposes increasing long-term development aid except in cases of East-West security considerations or as rewards for ideological loyalty. Congress tends towards using need, rather than strategic concerns, as the major criterion in determining the direction of economic assistance to Africa. Shepherd traces the circuitous routes of several food aid bills through the legislative process, faulting Congress for attaching domestic farm credit amendments as well as the Reagan administration for attaching amendments calling for military aid to the Contras.

Steketee, Richard W. Atlanta: Center for Disease Control, 26 February 1985.

Reports a 55 percent malnutrition rate at Fau. Suggests additional expatriate staffing and that priority be given to feeding and water purification programs.

Stephenopoulis, George. "Sudan Has Little Food for Stream of Ethiopian Refugees." *Christian Science Monitor*, 11 January 1985.

An update of the refugee crisis in the Sudan with emphasis on the food and water shortages at Tuklebab and Wad Kowli. The report also includes a discussion of the drought emergency in the Sudan itself.

Timm, Ian. Letter to IRC headquarters, New York, 26 December 1984.

A comprehensive description of the refugee crisis in eastern Sudan and of initial operations at Fau I. Even at this late date, Timm requests a staff of only 11 to 12 expatriates for the Fau camps.

United Nations High Commission for Refugees, Branch Office for the Sudan. *Briefing Note on Refugees in the Sudan.* Khartoum, The Sudan, 1 October 1985.

A 16-page document discussing refugees from Uganda into southern Sudan, refugees from Chad into western Sudan, but focusing on refugees from Ethiopia into eastern Sudan. It lists and describes program priorities as site selection, food supply and distribution, water supply and distribution, health, cholera prevention, shelter, and logistics. It includes a map of eastern Sudan refugee camps, a listing of UNHCR/Sudan staff, and a list of organizations assisting refugees in the Sudan.

Index